Mountain Words

Colin Brash

Chris Harle and Graham Wilson

MOUNTAIN WORDS

British hill and crag literature:
into the 21st century

Millrace

First published in Great Britain in 2009 by
Millrace
2a Leafield Road, Disley
Cheshire SK12 2JF
www.millracebooks.co.uk

ISBN: 978-1-902173-28-3

Typeset in Adobe Garamond Pro
Printed and bound in the United Kingdom
by T J International Ltd, Padstow, Cornwall PL28 8RW

Acknowledgements

I would like to thank all those who made it possible for me to produce the five essays that relate to recent British mountaineering literature. In particular, I would like to acknowledge the support and advice given by Ken Wilson and his permission to quote from his new edition of *Classic Rock*. As always, Ken has been most helpful and more than ready to put his considerable experience at my disposal.

I would also like to acknowledge the permission granted by Susan Steinberg to use her grandfather's photographs of Eagle's Nest Direct and John Cleare for the reproduction of his photograph of Crackstone Rib. Despite thorough investigation, I have been unable to contact the holder of the copyright of C D Milner's photograph of the Crack of Doom, which originally appeared in his classic collection *Rock for Climbing*. If notified, the publisher will be pleased to rectify any resultant errors or omissions at the earliest possible opportunity. Nevertheless, I would like to thank the various members of the Rucksack Club who tried to assist me in my search.

Finally, I was delighted to receive permission from Tom Price to quote his remarks about Moss Ghyll Grooves. Apparently he received my much-redirected postal request the day after his ninetieth birthday.

GW

About the Authors

CHRIS HARLE's passion for mountain literature was inspired by reading Buhl's *Nanga Parbat Pilgrimage*. Born in Kent in 1958 and educated in Essex and London, he escaped in 1981 to South Wales, where he fell out of love with football and in love with the mountains. For most of his working life, he has been involved in outdoor development training. He now lives in Matlock with his wife Jane and is the 'Bookman' for the Outside shops.

Mountain highlights over the last few years include completing a Coast to Coast across Scotland, an expedition to Chiring We (6559m) in the Indian Himalaya, adventure climbing in Jordan and a bivvy on the Cuillin Ridge.

GRAHAM WILSON's climbing career began on the crags of the North East in the 1950s but it was not until he retired as Head of English at the King's School in Macclesfield that he started to write about his long acquaintance with the British hills. Since then, he has had seven 'outdoor' books published, as well as a collection of short stories, a study of Shakespeare and an appraisal of English rugby. His book *A Rope of Writers* was short-listed for the Boardman Tasker Prize.

He is an ardent Sunderland supporter and was also for many years an English Schools rugby selector. He has lived in Macclesfield with his wife Tricia for over forty years.

Contents

An Explanation

We would like to explain at the outset that, although this book is inspired by W R Neate's *Mountaineering and its Literature* (1978) and its revision *Mountaineering Literature* (1986), it does not aspire to be a continuation. Indeed, as climbing literature is not exempt from the general increase in publishing mania, it would require a mightier tome than this to cover the ground. Instead, we decided to produce a bibliography that limited its ambition to books published in the twenty-five years between 1983 and 2008 which have their roots in climbing activity on British mountains. Five introductory essays are also included, with the intention of throwing some light on recent developments.

There are two more lists. The first is our choice of the fifty books which, prior to 1983, have made the most significant contribution to the literature of climbing in Britain. The second is of all books short-listed for the Boardman Tasker Prize. We include the latter in the hope it might give some idea of the number of recent climbing books of real worth—*Touching the Void* being an obvious example—that lie outside the scope of this work.

As we wanted to emphasise the literary content, we decided to exclude guidebooks, 'coffee table' collections of photographs and individual club journals unless they contained writing of either particular merit or historical significance. We have, probably, given greater prominence than Neate to books that deal with hill walking, as long as their primary concern is the mountain experience rather than exercising the dog. We felt that, both for the individual climber and the development of the sport, this branch of mountaineering has often been seminal.

The general format is as Neate: authors listed in alphabetical order with their works consecutively numbered. Each entry contains bibliographical details and, where needed, a thumbnail sketch of the contents. There is also an index of titles. Finally, for those who have found difficulty in locating a publication where they remembered the substance but neither author nor title in sufficient detail, we have included a Search by Category section that groups together works with a common factor, e.g. Biography, Munro-bagging. It is hoped that this facility will render any future quest for the half-remembered a little less likely to resemble a blind man looting a bazaar in a vain attempt to find his own portrait.

CH/GW

NOTE: In GW's essays, the H number following a book title is a cross-reference to CH's bibliography. A number preceded by the letter L means the book is to be found in the pre-1983 'Top Fifty' list.

1 The Future is in Blogs?

Why, from *Scrambles in the Alps* to *Touching the Void*, mountaineering has produced such a rich and varied canon of literature, treading every pathway and leaving no awkward lump of rock unturned, seems a complex question. Other sports and pastimes do occasionally produce nuggets of their own among the many manuals of ways to grip a golf club or the plethora of young footballers giving their followers the benefit of their ghost-writer's opinion, but nearly all books on climbing have something worth reading within their covers. Even the humble guidebook, more often than not, has some historical or scientific garnish to give spice to the plain fare of its main course. Traditionally, this was quite substantial. Archer Thomson's *Climbing in the Ogwen District* has interesting articles on the wildlife, legendary and otherwise, that inhabited the region—articles which, with the introduction and various addenda, cover forty percent of the 130 pages of text. The remainder is devoted to a rather wordy, albeit entertaining, description of the climbs, which in a modern version would take up a quarter of the space.

Thomson's approach set the fashion and both Geoffrey Winthrop Young and Menlove Edwards made a significant literary contribution with their personal input into the Climbers' Club guides to Lliwedd and Cwm Idwal. This lyrical and satirical writing would not have struck a false note with their readers, who had come to expect a few literary flourishes with their climbing material. From Dante to Ruskin, philosophical musings had been interspersed with reflections on mountains and mountaineering, to such an extent that Wilfred Noyce was able to compile a critical résumé of these collective thoughts under the title *Scholar Mountaineers*. A title that would appear somewhat incongruous if the proponents of the sport under discussion had been soccer players.

In fact, one of the main reasons for the quality of mountain writing is that the activity has traditionally attracted academics. In the 19th century, Oxbridge dons would conduct their reading parties in such areas as the Lake District and, on the principle that a lively mind flourished in a healthy body, the study of Ovid and Catullus was interspersed with invigorating tramps around the neighbouring hills. In a similar vein, Victorian scientists forsook the comfort of the valley to conduct their research in the natural sanctuary of the mountains, where scarce flora and fauna might flourish and the rocks offered unblemished geological evidence. If that meant scrabbling up vegetated gullies and along precarious ledges, then so be it. It was then their practice to deliver papers on their findings to like-minded colleagues which, for later reference, were gathered together in periodic Journals. When it came to recording their recreational activities in the hills, it is not surprising that they used the same format to record the days' events and in 1863 the first Journal of the Alpine Club appeared, which was to act as a model for all the following publications of more localised climbing clubs.

Of other sports, only cricket has a similar literary canon. As a pastime, it has obvious connections with mountaineering and it might help to answer the opening query if we consider what they are. Unlike the hurly-burly of football, for example, both take place over considerable periods of time, with suitable breathing spaces which give opportunity for reflection and considered thought. They are also activities where individuals operate as a team, yet each, paradoxically, is entirely reliant on his or her own efforts. The roles of an opening batsman facing a particularly fast bowler on a deteriorating pitch and an unprotected leader on steep unstable rock are strikingly similar. Not least because when they're out, they're out. Cricket also attracts its scholars or, at least, individuals with an enquiring and innovative mind, as is witnessed by the string of playwrights and musicians it can count among its fervent admirers. And, perhaps most significantly, both groups of sportsmen, at the close of play, spend time discussing the finer points of their game over a suitable beverage.

In addition, both sports collect and collate data in abundance. In the case of climbing, it is a matter of recording dates and personnel involved in first ascents, listing climbs in order of difficulty, compiling tables of hills, according to actual, comparative and relative height, then creating simple or complex formulae to determine whether a given point is indeed the true summit of a mountain or merely a subsidiary top. The equivalent in cricket is the sophisticated scorebook. In no other sport are the scorers such an integral part, as the results of their decisions will be regarded as a true testament of the game in question, both at the time and also in years to come.

An expert can, from a study of these figures and symbols, gauge the ebb and flow of a game and the parts that various players contributed to the outcome, as a conductor would read the pace and mood of a symphony from his musical score. In a similar fashion, climbers can 'read' a guidebook to identify the nature and difficulty of a climb they are planning to complete, or to dream of imagined glory on those that stray beyond the limits of their reasonable ambition. Nor is the desire to record exclusively the preserve of a few anoraks. Itineraries and logs usually allow space for personal addenda and there can scarcely be a copy of a climbing guide in circulation that does not bear witness to a series of cryptic symbols that record the owner's particular successes and failures.

The literary ways of the two sports seem to part company at this point. Cricket writing is, for the most part, retrospective, recalling great moments of triumph, disaster and controversy. Mountaineering has its fair share of 'blue remembered hills', but much of its literature, at least in its beginnings, was designed, consciously or otherwise, to encourage exploration of both new climbs and the limits of human endurance and skill. The bragging rights of one climber, no matter how modestly they were concealed, were little more than an implicit challenge to another to do better. At times, the challenge was far from implicit. When the controversy over the use of artificial aids was at its height, Maurice Linnell completed the first ascent of Overhanging Wall on the East Face of Scafell. At what turned out to be the crux, he placed a piton. His attitude was unequivocal:

I inserted a piton in the little crack and inserted it well and truly with a hammer. Nor was it only put there as a safeguard; by pulling on it sideways, downwards, outwards, and upwards, and finally planting a foot on it, I was able, with a struggle, to reach a little ledge. I offer no apologies. Those who prefer to climb the place unaided are cordially invited to remove the piton and do so.

Such challenges were not ignored. A year or so later, a group of climbers from Germany visited North Wales and completed a new route on the East Face of Tryfan which was christened Munich Climb in their honour. Three pitons, however, had been placed for protection and one was left on the crag. At the time, sullying British rock fell into the same category as shooting a fox, so a group of the Climbers' Club's most able was despatched to remove the offending ironmongery and climb the route 'free'. Their success was deemed to have saved British honour.

A record of such thrusts and counter-thrusts would find a permanent way into the Journals of the Clubs in question. This would explain why there was a ready source of material waiting to act as inspiration for a more considered analysis and literary expression. But it does not explain why club journals, as we now understand them, came into being. Why did a 'journal' become the 'Journal' and a 'club' become the 'Club'?

Mankind is a gregarious animal who, over the centuries, has evolved a series of activities, sporting, creative and intellectual, and therefore it is no surprise that like-minded groups congregated together. There was a variety of reasons for their formation, ranging from snobbery to economic interdependence, but from Boodles to the Co-op their purpose was the same: to recruit a membership that would use its enthusiasm and skills to encourage and sustain the continuance of its activity. As the 'Origin and Aims' of one now famous club put it: to provide 'possession of greater facilities for cultivating each other's friendship, also for opportunities to render mutual assistance in the enjoyable exercise of their sport'. In practice, this came to mean arranging 'Meets', providing Club centres and equipment, and leaving 'Climbing Books' at prearranged centres in which members could record descriptions of new climbs and expeditions.

All this information (quite apart from the inevitable reminder that subs were due) had to be disseminated and the easiest way was by some type of round robin, which took the form of the Journal. Yet this doesn't explain why these journals became such a force in the formation of literature that dealt with climbing in Britain. After all, once the original aims and purposes of the club had been explained in the first edition, its successors, to fulfil their basic function, could have been, after the usual editorial expostulations, little more than a bald statement of fact that included the necessary details of new climbs in the district, a list of members and the dates of future meets. To see what actually happened, it will probably pay dividends to examine in some detail early editions of that 'now famous' club. The Fell and Rock Climbing Club of the English Lake District, founded in 1907, produced the first of its literary outpourings at the end of that year.

It opened in an unusual fashion with an obituary. John Wilson Robinson was a local dalesman and held in high regard in Lake District climbing circles. His knowledge of the crags and gullies of his native fells

The Future is in Blogs?

was probably unparalleled and he was, in many ways, the English equivalent of John Mackenzie, the Scottish guide crofter who guided Collie and other Victorian pioneers through the maze of the Cuillin. Between 1882 and 1906 Robinson scaled Pillar Rock 101 times and reached the summit of Scafell Pinnacle over fifty. He completed these routes with both expert and tyro, and, moreover, with either sex. The climbs he helped to pioneer in a partnership with W P Haskett Smith that lasted two decades included Needle Ridge on the Napes and E Buttress on Dow Crag. He was present in Moss Ghyll when Collie hacked his infamous step in the rock with his ice axe and was in the party that made a famous winter ascent of Great Gully above the Wastwater Screes, reported in no less a publication than the Scottish Mountaineering Club Journal, which rarely strayed below the Highland Line. He was not left behind by the advances of the new generation, climbing with the Abraham Brothers and making new ascents with the legendary O G Jones. Not surprisingly, as it was the Club's avowed intent to introduce the locals to a sport that lay in their own backyard, Robinson was made Senior Vice-President of the Fell and Rock, but unexpectedly died before the first edition of its Journal had gone to print. A full account of his life, *A Lakeland Climbing Pioneer* (H237), was published in 2007.

Once these obsequial duties had been observed, the

real business began, which laid down a pattern that later editions were to follow. After explaining the climbing history of the district at some length, there were two individual accounts by experienced Club members, Messrs Woodhead and Botterill, of new climbs on Scafell and Pavey Ark and a full account of the established climbs on a lesser-known cliff, Gimmer Crag in Langdale. There followed book reviews, photographs, reports on the Meets and the inevitable Notes from the Committee. All very predictable, except for three additional articles.

The first, written by the President himself, Ashley Abraham, is entitled 'An Hour in the Smoke Room at Wasdale'. In it, an Old Stager rather mischievously goads the younger members of the Club into action. He suggests that they are doing little more than resting on the laurels of their forebears, content to climb well-trod routes, rather than seeking out new climbs for themselves. The younger members retort that their apparent lethargy is because their forebears have climbed all the rock that is climbable, leaving them no option but to repeat the existing courses. The reproof by the Old Stager takes the form of an apparent digression which tells how, when exploring the faces of Scafell, he had noticed a 'bayonet-shaped crack' on the great buttress that lay between Moss Ghyll and Botterill's Slab. It had suggested to him, he recalls, a possible weakness in a vast expanse of virgin rock.

His ploy must have worked as the next generation laid siege to the area until, just before the outbreak of the Great War, the renowned Central Buttress of Scafell was finally climbed.

At first glance, the other two articles could be mistaken for essays on the difficulties and dangers that a beginner might face when climbing on rock and snow. Closer examination shows that their central purpose was more to amuse and entertain. After all, if the President could adopt a quietly flippant tone, lesser mortals might follow. And, in due course, follow they did, casting aside any pretence of a more serious motive. Later articles entitled 'Stray Leaves' and 'A Midnight Climb' investigated the dubious pleasures of wild camping and climbing in the dark. They relied on the humour that is generated by the readers knowing the authors and, in the latter account, which was mildly iconoclastic, understanding the protocol and ethics of the Club. This set a tone for all Journals and humorous pieces of this type soon became commonplace, with such exponents as C F Holland, Menlove Edwards, G J F Dutton and Tom Patey each playing his part in the tradition.

If we return to the first Fell and Rock Journal, a careful inspection shows how it supported the 'Aims of the Club'. The Gimmer Guide and the new routes 'render[ed] mutual assistance in the enjoyable exercise of their sport', as did the Old Stager's veiled encouragement of further exploration to enhance the standing of the Club. The arranging of meets and amusing stories with their in-jokes helped to 'cultivat[e] each other's friendships' and the prominent position of the eulogy on Robinson indicated the sort of behaviour that was expected from Club members. This, along with a history now shared by all, was designed to cement the unspoken aim behind the Aims: the creation of an essential *esprit de corps*.

The pattern was followed in subsequent editions. There were occasional accounts of the fellow sports of pot-holing and fell running, and of the activities of members abroad, but a flick through the following years would reveal no startling changes. Historical accounts naturally diminished as members were eventually brought up to speed and, as the difficulty of travel eased, the accounts of foreign ventures became more ambitious, reporting success and failure from the greater ranges of the Himalayas and Andes. Yet an original member, picking up a current volume, would have little difficulty in recognising what he held in his hand. The familiar red cover, the sections on 'Climbs Old and New', Book Reviews and Obituaries of past members are still the staple diet. Humorous articles are still accepted, although the humour has adopted a harder edge and nowadays is not so much separated from the serious articles as intertwined within them.

As a result, climbing journals became a nursery bed for climbing literature at large. Neate lists more than thirty separate annual publications and that means that more than thirty editors must, at one time or another, have demanded, pleaded for or wheedled out copy to fill their pages. Some of these seedlings sprouted into more fully developed accounts of climbing experiences, which in turn inspired others to produce similar work of their own time. And so, between the twisting and twisted arm, an industry was born, based on a tradition of writing well and eschewing the easy short cuts of the hack. By and large, it took seriously what was serious and made fun of what was not.

One result of this continuity was that when suitable anniversaries came round, there was plenty of material from which a selection could be made. The Fell and Rock set the pace when they devoted their 1986 Journal (H60) to a celebration of the passing of a century since Walter Parry Haskett Smith first ascended the Needle. It was deemed a suitable moment for controlled nostalgia and the reprinting of articles on the first ascent of the Club's totem pole by the perpetrator and on its other glory, Herford's conquest of Scafell's Central Buttress, as recounted by G S Sansom. Any tendency to self-congratulation was tempered by the retelling of Graham Sutton's well-known short story 'The Man Who Broke the Needle' and a contemporary expert's tale of his trials and tribulations on CB.

Other collections followed and, not having such a symbolic moment to celebrate as the Fell and Rock with its Needle, had to rely upon chronological coincidence. The most obvious date was the founding of the Club, and in 1988 and 1997 respectively, the Scottish Mountaineering Club (H29) and the Climbers' Club (H92) published their centennial journals which comprised a selection of the best that had been produced over the years. They had, however, been beaten to it by the Rucksack Club, who put together an anthology of articles written for the journal under the title *From Kinder Scout to Kathmandu, a Rucksack Club Anthology 1907–1986* (H19). This differed from similar publications in two ways. First, it was not published to mark any celebratory date, but because the Club had been left some money which would help cover the cost of the print run and, second, as the title suggests, the Club's activities were widespread, not only geographically but also in the various types of hill activity undertaken.

As the Club was located in Manchester, it had equal access to both the Lakes and North Wales, so a range of British rock climbing was naturally included, from H M Kelly's history of Moss Ghyll Grooves through the irrepressible musings of Morley Wood on most things to P J Harding's self-deprecating account of the beginnings of his climbing career, ending at the point when he made the first ascent of Spectre on Clogwyn y Grochan. But, more unusually, the Club took an active interest in hill walking and a third of the selection was devoted to accounts of walks, long walks and, in some cases, very long walks completed in a very short time. Bog-trotting, i.e. ploughing around the peaty wastes of the Peak District hinterland, had long been a favourite activity of the Club and, as Derbyshire's boundaries were soon encompassed, ambitions grew. The final piece in the selection is an account by Mike Cudahy of his successful attempt to complete the Pennine Way in three days. As a warm-up for this 270-mile marathon, Cudahy broke his own record for Tan Hill to the Cat and Fiddle, completing the 120 miles in 29 hours, 10 minutes. On 3rd June 1984 he broke the three-day barrier, where even the renowned Joss Naylor had failed, in a time of two days, 21 hours, 54 minutes, 30 seconds.

Manchester had another string to its bow. The *Manchester Guardian* had taken an interest in the development of climbing in Britain from its very beginnings and the paper continued to do so when it dropped its parochial prefix. Given its original readership, it first concentrated its attention on the developments taking place in the Peak District and the Lakes but later expanded its remit. It is probably impossible to gauge whether the paper set out to attract mountain writers or these same writers gravitated towards a paper that they trusted. The response of the average journo is to pump up any Everest-type triumph and be equally quick to brand as foolish and irresponsible any mountaineer who is unfortunate enough to meet with an accident. So, for climbers, the *Manchester Guardian* was a refreshing change. Whatever the chicken and egg, the outcome was that, with an editorial tradition run by men like C P Scott, Patrick Monkhouse and Alastair Hetherington, mountain-lovers all, the paper was able to attract writers of the quality of C E Montague, Harry Griffin and Jim Perrin. These professionals set and maintained standards that served climbing literature well.

The paper was also willing to take up the cudgels in any climbing controversy. There were leaders on Access and the Right to Roam, the ethics of artificial aids, particularly as they applied to the argument of climbing being hijacked to bolster national prestige, and more recently the desirability of climbing competitions.

In particular, the paper took up the case of women climbers. In 1921 a group led by Eleanor Winthrop-Young and 'Pat' Kelly wrote to announce the inaugural meeting of the Pinnacle Club, to be set up exclusively for women. To their delight, not only was their letter published but followed by a leading article supporting the project, written by no less a person than C E Montague himself. Thereafter articles regularly appeared arguing the women's case and highlighting the indignities to which they had been traditionally subjected. In 1998, Ed Douglas wrote a piece about the rights and wrongs of mothers with small children undertaking difficult and potentially dangerous climbs. The popular press has always been excited by the idea of *Mums in Peril!!!* but when the peril is self-inflicted, as in Alison Hargreaves' death on K2, it releases the full force of its furies. *The Times* joined the other tabloids in a predictable rant, with Nigella Lawson using such emotive phrases as 'me-first mountaineering' and 'brutally ignoring' responsibilities. *The Guardian* allowed the voice of the woman climber to be heard and made the point that, if the cases in question had concerned fathers, little or nothing would have been said.

The *Guardian* pieces have been gathered together chronologically in *The Guardian Book of Mountains* (H168). As a result, the reader can trace the history and traditions of the sport through thoughtful obituaries and accounts of new climbs. In the last respect, the paper was particularly fortunate to employ two climbers, David Rose and Roger Alton, whose understanding of what lay behind the hard new routes of the Eighties enabled *The Guardian*, unlike some of its rivals, to keep in touch with life after Joe. Any of the articles, from Harry Griffin's contributions to 'A Country Diary' to 'Everest beaten—the hard way', an assessment of the successful British ascent of the south-west face by Ken Wilson, could have found its way into one of the established Journals of their day.

But the moving finger writes and having writ moves

on, and neither Piety nor Will could stop the advance of the electronic keyboard. Suddenly the Journal began to look rather old-fashioned. Those who, as a new Millennium approached, climbed, aspired to climb or merely applauded the efforts of others on the new über-routes, were little more used to carefully constructed sentences and finely wrought figures of speech than to routes that mention chimneys, chockstones and Thank God holds. They liked their prose, as they liked their climbs, bald, brutish and to the point (preferably at least red) and the chances were that sooner rather than later they would kick against the traces.

Oddly enough, it was again the 'humble guidebook' that set the pace. It was generally agreed that the senior Clubs had ownership of the official and definitive list of climbs in their area and the responsibility for appointing a writer whose job it was to describe and grade them. The quid pro quo was the Club's obligation to keep the list up to date. In this respect, Borrowdale became a particular running sore. Previously, apart from a few classics like Sergeant Crag Gully and Troutdale Pinnacle, the valley had been of little interest to the climber. Although Bentley Beetham had put up scores of routes for instructional purposes, they were for the most part a series of short pitches, often separated, in rock climbing terms, by a lengthy walk.

Then, in the late Fifties, matters changed dramatically. Because the rocks were low-lying, they were swathed with vegetation, but once this was removed a number of fine steep walls were revealed. The partnerships of first Pete Greenwood and Paul Ross, and then Ross and Pete Lockey, explored this steeper rock that had never been tackled before and by the mid Sixties hard routes of the calibre of Post Mortem on Eagle Crag and Dedication on Falcon Crag had appeared. The news spread and Borrowdale became the place to be, with a frantic scramble for the remaining plums. Obviously, all this activity meant a demand for a new guide, but the Fell and Rock seemed in no hurry to do anything about it. So Ross and Mike Thompson produced one of their own.

This act of *lèse-majesté* caused more than a ripple, particularly as the co-authors had decided unilaterally to alter the hallowed grading system by dividing the VS grade into three by adding the suffixes (easy) and (hard), and throwing in an extra Extremely Severe category. They also refused to produce a classified list of climbs on the grounds that such lists were a load of nonsense. What is more, the old guide was given short shrift. Many of Bentham's discoveries were ignored and routes like Ashness Ghyll, which previously had been described as 'a thoroughly worthwhile expedition', were now dismissed as 'uniquely revolting'. Player power had arrived.

The implications were significant. If guidebooks could be produced independently to meet demand, then the Club's 'Climbs Old and New' could become redundant—and 'Climbs Old and New' was a central pillar that supported the importance of the Journal. The late 20th-century arrival of desktop publishing and the internet with its websites and blogs has given another kick to that pillar and it seems as if first the official guides, then the Journals and finally the Clubs themselves could fade and wither on the vine.

But even if blogs win OK, there is no reason to believe that the keyboard should be less mighty than the pen. There is a possible debate about the question of permanent record but it may turn out that material freely available to the many has quite the value of expensively produced information limited to the few. Until the former becomes buried in an avalanche of manuals that instruct you how to make progress by putting one foot in front of the other and what to do if you meet a barbed-wire fence, or Munro-bagging becomes the new football, thoughtful comment should always prevail.

Of course, as with any populist activity, it might spawn a literati, weaned at the established universities sponsored by Pete's Eats, whose sole scholarly ambition is to reduce the delightful vagaries of the traditional guidebook to an ever-increasing combination of definitive numbers with alphabetical subdivisions.

Vids 'n' Verbs

On the walls in what was the dining room, now covertly converted into my library, are three photographs of rock climbers in action. The climbs in question are Eagle's Nest Direct on the Napes, taken by the Abraham Brothers, the Crack of Doom on Sron na Ciche by C D Milner, and Crackstone Rib on Carreg Wastad by John Cleare. They represent three very early climbs I did, each having its own evocation. The Eagle's Nest Direct picture was on the wall of the Wasdale Head Hotel dining room and acted as a breakfast inspiration every morning of my first climbing holiday; the Crack of Doom was the epitome and height of all the history and literature that surrounded the Cioch and such godfather figures as Dr Collie, the Abrahams and W H Murray; and Carreg Wastad was in the Pass which was, in those days, muttered in the blasphemously reverential terms that, no doubt, were once reserved for a similar *mauvais pas* in the Hindu Kush. The remaining walls of my room are coated with shelves of which a significant number contain books on mountaineering. These range from the prosaic guidebook to the more highly wrought catalogues of memory and opinion. From time to time the question passes my mind—whether one picture *is* worth a thousand words when it comes to describing a climb.

Closer examination shows that my pictures are more than memoranda of times past. Each of the visual images relays additional information and, to a greater or lesser extent, reflects the attitudes of the age in which it was taken. In the first (Plate 1), the image of the climber, a couple of moves away from stepping up onto the security of the belay ledge, underlines the mores of late Victorian society. There is an air of control and co-ordination, with the rope linking the second to his indistinguishable leader held firmly, yet not taut, which suggests co-operative teamwork based on an understood sense of protocol and hierarchy. The Norfolk jacket and plus fours were as *de rigueur* as any formal morning or evening attire. Contemporary writers deplored a lack of proper attention to dress or, as Claude E Benson complained, a 'Weary Willie appearance'. The ominous snow-clad background and the exposed drop that surround the climber suggest that the achievement, like that of the Empire, was a well-planned victory against the odds.

In the second (Plate 3), the subject of the photograph is now the leader, whose rope leads from an invisible second. Again, there is a feeling of control and concentration but on this occasion the head is upturned, suggesting that he is involved in the exploration of new territory rather than treading in the steps of those who have gone before. The change from snow to sun makes the action seem less spartan and more athletic, and the more casual dress suggests a holiday mood. There is a sense of isolation and apartness that was typical of the long, unprotected run-outs of the time, of which the most renowned was the unseen lead by Colin Kirkus on the Great Slab of Clogwyn du'r Arddu, trailing 100 feet of hemp line behind him.

In the final picture (Plate 4), a darkened figure silhouetted against a lightened sky simultaneously offers opposing images. It has the feel of an end of an era, with the sun going down on a golden age of British rock climbing. An era where the climber was unencumbered by helmet and harness and the movement was more akin to a performance on the dance- rather than the gym-floor. Or it could be the beginning of a different age, the figure as striking as the islands rising starkly out of a dawn-struck sea. The detail is indiscernible, the figure has no individuality; it is an Everyman trapped in some constant cycle.

And, in these respects, the photographs show that sport mimics the real world. The early climbers' efforts were truly co-operative; human pyramids, based on a developed understanding of engineering and mechanics, were formed to overcome otherwise unassailable difficulties. The apotheosis of that particular period, the ascent of the Great Flake on the Central Buttress of Scafell, was just such a case. The metaphor was one on which the Empire was built and in which the needless sacrifice of the Great War was rooted. The informality

Plate 1: Eagle's Nest Direct
© abraham photographic

Plate 2: Eagle's Nest Direct
© abraham photographic

Plate 3: Crack of Doom
© C Douglas Milner

Plate 4: Crackstone Rib
© John.Cleare/www.mountaincamera.com

of dress and the unprotected run-out in the second picture are not unconnected with the paradoxical freedom that economic depression gave an unemployed working class who, unfettered by convention, pushed back the barriers in more ways than one. In the final picture, we see the hinge of climbing history, when advancements in safety technique encouraged bolder and more technically demanding moves and reflected both the popularist existentialism of 'doing your own thing' and the technological innovations that characterised the second half of the 20th century. Even the shift in the photographers' names from formal address to first-name terms underlines the various stages of social change.

But pictures, as well as revealing truth, can also lie or, at least, misrepresent. As John Berger points out in his *Ways of Seeing*, all images are shaped by the received culture of the observer. (Most advertisements rely on a setting that makes the potential buyer wish it was he or she who were the owner of the items in question, so you don't place bejewelled women in a dark threatening alley or cigar smokers in a cancer ward, rather at a glittering social occasion or an opulent gentleman's club.) A pertinent example is the well-known image of the Vietnamese child, ablaze with burning napalm, running along a track towards the camera. It seems to be a protest against the atrocities committed by the USA in the name of democracy and designed to outrage a civilised world into a similar and greater protest. But is what we see the whole truth? Could not the photographer have abandoned his camera to help the child? Could there be alternative, commercial motives for taking the shot? Would it make any difference if there was a battery of cameramen vying for the best angle? If any of this were true, it would seriously confuse the apparently intended message. Even if the child was too far away to be saved and a zoom lens was necessary to get the shot at all, or the lone cameraman had no possible means of putting the fire out, or you believe that the journalist's job is to record so that others can judge, I, at least, felt uncomfortable as to what was actually going on.

I am not suggesting that all professional pictures are as confusing as that, but I am suggesting that they are arranged for effect and that 'art' has more than one meaning. The Abrahams' photograph under discussion (Plate 1) is an interesting case in point. There is no doubt that for me the main attraction of the image was the insouciance, the poise and indifference to danger caught in the photograph. It turns out that this picture was but one of a series. I discovered, some time later, in Alan Hankinson's *Camera on the Crags* (L18), another print of the climb taken by the Abrahams (Plate 2). It is clearly the same 'shoot'. It is the same climber, in the same clothes, taken from the same viewpoint against the same background. Yet the image differs significantly from my original. Although the climber is more or less at the same point, he is not in the same position. His weight is distributed differently. As a result, there is less weight on his feet and his body is held in place by friction from his arms and left knee. In the 'Wasdale Dining Room' photograph, the weight has been placed over the feet and consequently arms and knee are not required to maintain contact with the rock. There is the air of a man who has completed a tricky task with care and without fuss. The rope is a symbol of unity, not a potential aid to progress. I am not saying that previously he was flailing around like a fish on a line, but it is probably true to say that, at that very moment, he was quite happy he was not leading.

Given that this was before the days of digital snap-happiness, and taking into account the problems involved in operating a plate camera while balancing a tripod on a precarious ledge, it would suggest that the Abrahams were not happy with their first shot. The brothers were a commercial outfit and they wanted to take photos that the public would buy. If the current myth was centred around heroic exploration of the unknown, then that is what they sought to create. In a similar way, John Cleare freely admitted to tilting the camera on the grounds that, although that might not be as it is, it is how it seems to the climber. Even the most inexperienced of happy-snappers tend to remove signs of civilisation from their vistas of the 'Last Wilderness'. The problem with this approach is that it creates doubt in the mind of the beholder. If the cameraman can place the subject to suit his needs, did he ever climb the route at all or was he simply lowered into position? Has *anyone* ever climbed Eagle's Nest Direct? Did the Americans really land on the moon? Such doubts undermine the very *raison d'être* of the photograph as truthful reporter.

As explained, the room's remaining walls are partially covered with books on mountaineering. They too have to bear their share of scrutiny as to which is the more effective portrayal of what climbing is about. First, it must be allowed that words are no more honest than pictures. The mixture of Anglo-Saxon and Norman French allows intentional ambiguity to flourish. There is no difference, yet a world of difference between 'cooking' and 'cuisine'. Irony which assumes the reader is capable of reading at more than one level is abundant and no more than a glance at the tabloids will show how easy it is to manipulate the meaning of words. Nor, to add to the general confusion, is the visual image necessarily of a different order to the literary one. At the height of the debate, when radio was on the cusp of being replaced by television, a child was asked which of the two she preferred. She replied, 'The radio, because it has the better pictures.'

And so, if it's not a question of truth, it must be a question of suggestion. Which does produce the more effective image in the mind, the photograph or the written description? If we were to concentrate on the Crack of Doom as a subject and compare an example from each media, it might be possible to reach some conclusion. At the outset, the written word scores an unexpected point. The phrase *Crack of Doom* is instantaneously both informative and emotive, invading the very area of immediacy that should be the prerogative of the camera. But the quality of the effect is open to question. Is it too close to melodrama for comfort? If, when experienced, the climb fails at the first hurdle of expectancy, the description could appear risible and it would no more compete with a dramatic photograph than does the SMC's guidebook description of the route which, after spending four lines describing the various approaches to the foot of the climb, expends merely seven words on a description that informs the reader that the crack gets steeper near the top. Fortunately, there is better evidence to be called in the defence of literature.

W H Murray, in his book *Mountaineering in Scotland* (L28), writes an account of the climb. After a prelude that offers an overview of the difficulties to be encountered, the piece is in five movements that develop as the climber ascends the route. In the first and easiest section, the emphasis is on a combination of balance and neatness that allows the climber to cover the ground with the minimum expenditure of energy. This is followed by a passage of rest, when not only physical but also mental energy is recharged as Murray gains strength from the reassuring presence of his trusted second and memories of past successes gained in more adverse conditions. In stage three, the tone changes and the Crack itself begins to take a more challenging part in the drama. The fissure narrows and the holds grow smaller and further apart. No longer is the climber in easy control. Fate, moreover, threatens to intervene in the shape of faulty equipment. Words and phrases like *fight, force, pressure hold* and *clenched fist* intrude into the description and indicate that a struggle has begun to develop. So that in the fourth stage the outcome is uncertain until the inner resources of determination and self-esteem come into play. The climb responds. The final overhanging obstacle is a *tongue of stone* that *mocks* [his] *weariness*. The climber counters with *grasp, heave, swarm* and, amidst a triumphant change of key, hauls himself, tired yet victorious, to safety.

The Unities of Time, Place and Action, coupled with the rise and fall of emotion, suggest a classical drama. So it is interesting to discover how photographers, predisposed to composition, measure up in their rendering. Milner's construction (Plate 3) shows the rope leading the eye from bottom right to the dominant figure top left. It, in turn, is sufficiently off-centre to emphasise the upward movement of the climber, and the bars of dark shadow across the lightened gabbro suggest barriers that have been surmounted but also the possibility that more of a similar nature are yet to come. The sky at the top of the picture presents contradictory images. On the one hand, it is the top and comparative safety. On the other, there is also a sense of infinite space, a never-ending route. The Crack of Doom itself stands, a little ominously, in the wings.

So, in the end, the 'truth' is all a matter of what or how you see. Berger draws a sharp distinction between the young child who 'sees' objects and events within their own context as opposed to the adult who sees the same thing in an historical perspective. Hence, the pantomime villain is frightening to the child but not to its mother. Murray sees the climb in more than one tense. Although he describes the climb as it affected him at the time, this moment of description is framed by remembrance of past success and anticipation of what is to come. Additionally, the reader who is aware of the book's back story—that it was written when the author was a German prisoner of war—can put the struggle into another perspective.

Milner's photograph is more firmly set in the present. We have no knowledge of its prelude nor of the outcome. The immediate is paramount: how to use the combination of holds available to gain the next few inches. Once that move is made, the same situation is reformed with another set of holds and another puzzle to be solved. This is another present, another picture. The past no longer plays a part. The future is unknown.

In 1986 Johnny Dawes set out to attempt a new route on the Great Wall of Clogwyn du'r Arddu which he was to name Indian Face. Such holds as there were, were small and often awkwardly situated. At one point he reached a small ledge, sufficiently large to take his weight on his heels and rest his muscles. Here he stayed motionless for half an hour. *The Guardian* reported that such was his concentration on the difficulties to come that when he recognised an acquaintance on an adjacent climb he did not dare to raise even a smile in recognition. Any photograph of the solitary figure marooned in its frozen sea of rock would be a very powerful image of that particular 'present'. But there is an argument that the sentence from the newspaper's description is just as compelling in bringing the true situation into sharp focus. I suppose it's all a question of how you see it. Back to the little girl and her radio.

It could be contended that, as climbs become more and more difficult, a written description becomes ever more redundant. If a full description of a route is no more than 'Climb a smooth, shallow groove at sustained 6b rising to occasional 6c for 50m until the climber reaches a poor rest before tackling the final unprotected 12m of overhanging wall on friable holds at E12 7z', there is little you can add and any photograph or series of photographs would be more striking than additional words. There are few surprises to give the writer imaginative scope. What you see is what you get. When the rock architecture is such that the route might be anywhere, it is hard for the writer to engage the climber/reader as to the nature of the climb. So, perhaps, the author has to adopt another tack. A possible alternative is seen in the Climbers' Club 2004 guide to Clogwyn du'r Arddu. The relatively stark route descriptions are enhanced by an anthology that brings not only the climbs but also the surrounding circumstances to light. Indian Face was a culmination of two decades of looking and ambition. The nature of the comments by Dawes, Redhead and Towse, together with the semi-facetious article in *High*, tell you more about that central lump of rock face than any type of route description or topos with white lines chalked on them.

Perhaps this is the future for all guidebooks. Traditionally they existed because amateur enthusiasts gave up their time. Now it could be the turn of the professionals to enlarge on the idea suggested by *Rock Climbers in Action in Snowdonia* (L40), where the lively writing of Tony Smythe and John Cleare's subtly-composed images capture the nature of Welsh climbs and climbing in the Sixties. Ken Wilson's series from *Classic* to *Extreme Rock* could act as a model. Originally inspired by the work of André Roch and, interestingly enough, Milner, who combined their pictures with written commentaries, Wilson decided to juxtapose photographs with parallel words, and *Classic Rock* (H255) was given a refurb in 2007 when a new edition appeared. As a number of the original contributors had died, it was decided to leave the text virtually unchanged. There is a nod towards how improved protection can make the likes of Main Wall on Cyrn Las less serious and further analysis on the subject of grading but, by and large, well has been left alone. The real difference is in the new set of photographs. Now for the most part in colour, many of the climbs are seen with a fresh eye. There is an added sharpness, not only as a result of improved photographic techniques but also because there seems to have been a more concerted search for better photogenic opportunities. With illustrated endpapers and additional topographical detail, this is in no sense a reprint or even a fresh edition. It is, for practical puposes, a new book for a new century.

Nevertheless, I am pleased that the parallel commentaries have not been changed. They were written by a variety of authors who showed 'an air of restraint and maturity that perhaps reflected the more relaxed nature of the climbing'. In addition to technical detail, they encapsulate the history of the sport and the variety of location and rock architecture, while a sense of good humour and wit abound. As Tom Price so precisely put it in his account of Moss Ghyll Grooves, on a Classic Climb you can 'experience the excitement of vertical rock without the inconvenience of being out of balance'.

The commentaries range from accounts by first ascensionists to the thoughts of established mountain writers like Showell Styles and Jim Perrin. One, by Dave Cook, concerns my third picture, Cleare's Crackstone Rib (Plate 4). The Three Cliffs, poised several hundred feet above the narrow Llanberis Pass and surrounded to the south by the bulk of the Snowdon massif, offer splendid photo-opportunities and Cleare spectacularly seized the chance. A phrase that has always caught my imagination is 'on the edge of all things' and of all the pictures I have seen, Cleare's Crackstone Rib most closely equates with the image these words create in my mind. I was intrigued to see how Cook went about connecting the two. The problem he faced was to find a way to express the sensation that the camera had captured. In the end, he chose a story and, as many stories before it, it was a tale of a boy and a girl. The setting was Carreg Wastad and the moral of the tale was that he didn't know as much as he thought he did and she discovered that it's not so much a question of ribs but how you crack the stone. The villain, or probably the fairy godmother, of the piece was the weather.

They had been climbing all week on the south side of the Pass. He riding the 'escalator' of his ambition on climbs that were beyond her ability. She, as all the routes she was capable of leading were 'slimy side-shows', was hauled up along with the rest of the gear. From precarious stances she looked longingly across at the friendly, at times sunlit crag on the other side of the A4086. And that was how things stood between them. Then one morning it threatened to rain and, fearing a slip-up in his vaulting ambition, he agreed to let her lead Crackstone Rib, with a covert plan to save his face with Erosion Groove if the sun came out.

She led the first two pitches as one and the peak of exhilaration was reached as she stepped astride the rib. There was no way she was going to surrender the lead now and swiftly tied him to the belay 'like a novice', as he had so often done to her. At the finish, any thoughts of Erosion were dissolved by the now heavy rain and her enthusiasm to continue, this time on Wrinkle. For the first time the true pleasure of climbing dawned. It wasn't just the rib, the 'hinge' on which everything swung, but also the responsibility of the leader to 'judge, protect and not to fail'. That night together matters changed as the 'tight ropes that had pulled her not only as his second [...] but just as surely in the bar' slackened into mutual satisfaction and understanding. And, as far as we know, they lived happily ever after.

As with much of the rest of sporting life, the gap between the highest level of achievement and that of the general climbing public has widened to such an extent that most of us have no option but to watch the video. The tradition had been to work steadily through the grades until you reached your level. The VS leader was held in respect but on a good day, with the wind behind you, there was always a chance that you could step into the grade. For such was the elasticity of the VS cohort that the difference between top and bottom was probably greater than between the average Diff and the hardest Severe. Scrabbling around on Glyder Fach's Alpha was not quite in the same order of things as a sight lead of Suicide Wall, but you, as a 'VS man', could always pretend that it was.

Thatcherism produced an unexpected bonus in the form of a rise in standards. The stars may still have rubbed shoulders with the common herd in Pete's Eats but only in the sense that the Thirties football fan had shared the same tram as his heroic centre forward. Now, as instant fame and money is the name of the game, the written word is falling out of fashion, to be replaced by sound- and sight-bites. Public institutions are cutting back on books and spending more on DVDs; there are reports of schools shutting down their libraries and sacking specialist staff, and public libraries reducing their budget on children's books. The reaction of the author Philip Pullman was to complain that reading, instead of being the centre of the curriculum, is now reduced to an after-school option, with the same status as stamp collecting or Frisbee throwing. The vids seem to be shuffling into pole position and the verbs may have to look to their laurels.

A Stroll in the Park

During discussions as to what was and was not relevant to our undertaking, the place of 'walking' in the mountain literary canon was the most debated. In the end, the substance of the argument centred around whether books on walking in the hills should be included in a bibliography of mountaineering. In other words, whether walking is a valid subset of mountaineering. In the eyes of the general public, it is probably not. After all, walking is something we all do, but climbing (a term often synonymous with 'mountaineering') appears to require a different and probably superior set of skills.

Yet closer examination shows they have much in common. Both occur in remote places where the participants strive to reach a recognisable summit. Both use limbs rather than a machine for propulsion when making the necessary upward progression and both record their achievements and write guides for others to follow. There is a common essential skill in that the key to success is an eye for a route, coupled with an obsession with obtaining the most appropriate type of gear. Both are dangerous *per se* in that participants get killed or injured as a result of their own decisions. And, a clinching debating point, both are often to be found in particular public houses at the same sort of time.

The counter to these arguments is that, while they are true as they stand, they are syllogistically false, as in: a cat has four legs, a dog has four legs, so all dogs are cats. Essentially, mountaineering demands skills in climbing rock, snow and ice that are not a prerequisite for the simple trekker and while it would probably be admitted that a significant proportion of success on the greater ranges depends upon the virtues of stamina and determination, such a claim cannot be made for the less demanding British hills. Hamish Brown's account of how, as a young man, he walked in a continuous loop on the Ochils to see how far he could go before exhaustion set in could be cited as evidence that the sport of walking is little more than going round in circles.

What is more, the opposer could argue that, despite some superficial similarities, there is a quantum leap (whatever that might be) between one activity and another. First, the use of superficially similar equipment actually differs. With climbing it is proactive: selecting the right tools for the job; with the walker it is reactive: 'It's started to rain so I'd better put my woolly hat on.' And second, that perfecting the art of moving safely in dangerous places acquires greater significance to the climber than to the walker. It is possible that a dam wall might collapse and that the released avalanche of water could sweep you to your death, but it is unlikely that this possibility would be foremost in the mind of a man walking his dog along a canal towpath.

Such caustic comments on his art might force the walker to retreat into a corner, clutching his pint tankard of Scuttlethwaites Old Dementia and muttering that until trekking poles turn into pogo sticks he, at least, can manage without an assortment of pulleys to get him over every minor difficulty and the only greater danger that climbers really face is drowning in their own bullshit.

So there matters remained as a stalemate, but these are politically correct times and in a spirit of live and let live, we, in principle, allowed walkers and climbers to cojoin in this project and, to no one's particular surprise, they turned out to be good bedfellows.

Even assuming you allow books on walking into the mountaineering canon, there remains the question as to whether they have any significant literary value or are merely a how and where. The obvious start was to see what Neate had decided. The 1986 edition had included Hamish Brown and his Munro round and, more obviously from the climbers' point of view, Martin Moran's similar journey in winter. But, in the main, writing that dealt primarily with hill walking in Britain was thin on the ground. There was no mention, for example, of the early writings of A H Griffin about his beloved Lake District or Alfred Wainwright's literary and pictorial opera.

The former is particularly difficult to understand. If you were to take together *Inside the Real Lakeland* and

In Mountain Lakeland, you would have a more than adequate and well written account of the nature of rock climbing in the district, supplemented by its ancillary activities such as fell running and record-breaking peak bagging. Moreover, the account has depth as well as sweep. Climbing is regarded from an historical perspective; character sketches of famous climbers and their achievements and lively descriptions of key climbs are included. There are chapters that are extraneous to the actual act of climbing but, unless you believe that mountaineering consists entirely of titanic struggles conducted exclusively in wastelands of vertical rock and ice, then you will probably agree that the sympathetic pieces on Herdwick sheep and 'Auld Will Ritson' enhance rather than detract from your understanding of what is actually going on. I always felt that Griffin stood as a natural successor to Oppenheimer, whose *The Heart of Lakeland* (L30) is not only included but additionally 'starred' in Neate's first edition.

The case for Wainwright's exclusion is easier to understand. If 'mountaineering' must include at least the possibility of rock climbing, then Wainwright puts his own case out of court. As Griffin observed, AW viewed the coiled rope as if it were a coiled snake. Dire warnings are issued against going anywhere near Broad Stand and although Jack's Rake and Sharp Edge are admitted as possible ways for the pedestrian, they are served with a similar caveat to that which once came with the likes of Eagle's Nest Direct: 'For experts only and then only on a fine day in rubbers.' In addition, much of Wainwright's writing consists of guidebooks, which don't usually fall into the category of literature. They belong to the province of Do It Yourself Manuals along the lines of Mrs Beeton or the *Readers' Digest Guide to Motor Mechanics*.

But that does not mean Wainwright had no literary ambitions beyond his guidebook writing. He described his *Lakeland Pictorial Guides* as a 'love letter', which suggests a loftier aim, and there is more than sufficient circumstantial evidence that he harboured serious literary hopes from an early stage. He started at least one novel and in 1938 set off on another project, planning a two-week walking holiday in the Northern Pennines and Yorkshire Dales. It began at Settle, presumably because it was handy for Blackburn, and followed a route up the east side through Buckden, Keld and Blanchland to finish at Hadrian's Wall (because *that* was the end of the Pennines), then returned down the west by way of Alston, Appleby and Dent. He lodged at farmhouses or similar, and, carrying no change of clothes, was able to restrict the weight of his rucksack to no more than 2lbs. The route was of his own invention, created no doubt during many evenings poring over maps. There were five of these in all, covering the required area from east to west and south to north. He found this adjacency particularly useful for, in addition to enabling identification of old friends from new angles, he was able to correlate his northern and southern progress.

During his journey he kept a diary, took spools of photographs and produced a few sketches which, in the form of postcards, were sent to friends. When he returned, he set about turning his thoughts and recollections into a book that he planned to call *A Pennine Campaign*. The working title was misleading. It was in no way similar to the campaign he was later to wage in the Lake District, a campaign as thoroughly planned and executed as any of Caesar's. This record was very different from the writings with which the name Wainwright is usually associated, and the eventual title *A Pennine Journey* (H232), published nearly half a century later, is nearer the truth. It has little resemblance to his later detailed route descriptions, supported by meticulous drawings. Rather, it is an account of the people he met, peppered with views, at times perceptive, at times annoyingly sweeping, on life in general and women in particular.

Wainwright saw himself not only as a writer but also, in due course, as a published author. He passed the manuscript around his friends and attached what appeared to be a publishers' blurb followed by a cod review in which he compares the author, i.e. himself, not unfavourably with J B Priestley. While there is no doubt it was also intended to amuse its recipients, it is quite possible, as his biographer Hunter Davies observes, that he hoped that one of them might have had the ear of a Real Publisher. Events, however, intervened. But his life might have taken a very different turn if the manuscript had been taken up at that time and not after he had achieved his guidebook fame.

A close examination of the text shows that his book had literary ambitions, and publication would have given ample encouragement to other aspiring walker/writers. The language is heightened, if at times a little unnecessarily, to give colour and depth to his descriptions and his account of an ensnared rabbit writhing in agony is a revealing insight into one of the rites of passage that the townie has to undergo while learning to accept the harsher reality of his postcard countryside. The literary dynamic between the author, the rabbit and the approaching poachers, if not fully realised, has genuine quality. There is a tendency to explain rather than show. But in the dramatic account of the 'Great Flood' and his own consequent misfortunes, he puts a firm brake on any inclination towards melodrama.

Despite 'First catch your rabbit', *A Pennine Journey* is certainly not Mrs Beeton and, as I have already suggested, the quality of the writing is superior to much that passes as mountain literature. Yet there is a fatal flaw. If it is to compete with, say, *Mountaineering in Scotland*, there must be some sort of assault on high ground. There is scarcely a hill in sight; those that do appear are background colour rather than part of the challenge and he rarely rises to any particular eminence. Lack of footpaths and private ownership force a detour around the moors between the Tees and the Tyne. Desperate weather and flooded fields, with consequent delay (no throwing a sickie in those days), meant that much of the return leg had to be completed on tarmac. Even the planned ascent of Cross Fell, the highest hill in England outside the Lake District, had to fall victim to sensible prudence. Although there were higher points, his account reads as though High Shield Crag on Hadrian's Wall was not only the height of his ambition but near enough as high as he climbed.

A number of Wainwright's days were long and arduous. The route from Ronaldkirk to Blanchland approached thirty miles and took him around eleven hours. But he was by no means the first to spend, then write about, long days and nights in the hills. On 20th July 1923, the Revd Ronald Burn climbed the two tops of Beinn a' Chroin and, in so doing, completed an ascent of all the hills in Scotland that were then included in Munro's tables of mountains and their subsidiary tops, 558 in all. As he stated in the SMC Journal of that year, he believed that he was the first and only one 'to have done everything'. Another divine, A E Robertson, had been the first person to complete the table of separate mountains in 1901 and, by the time another hundred had joined him, less than a third of that number could measure their achievement with that of Burn. To put his undertaking into perspective, the next cohort of a hundred, despite improved travelling conditions, could only manage fourteen 'compleat' ascents between them.

What made his achievement all the more remarkable was that for much of the time Burn was based in Newmarket, only moving up to Glasgow in 1922. He was an unprepossessing man, short in stature and with a deformed back, but was a prodigious walker. Even at the end of a long day he strode out tirelessly, on one occasion, at the end of a trip from Loch Hourne to the Clunie Inn, covering the final one and a half miles at an average speed of six miles an hour. As he did not always follow the quickest route (he had a propensity for missing trains and losing his way), there is no doubt that this particular physical attribute played a significant part in his eventual success. He kept detailed records of routes taken and times spent on various legs, which he entered carefully into his notebooks. His greatest ambition was to be elected a member of the Scottish Mountaineering Club, to rub shoulders with the likes of Raeburn and Ling, and he hoped that his achievement would be his entrée. Probably less in his mind was that he was recording vital information for his hill-walking biography and about the nature of life in the Glens around the turn of the 19th century.

In 1995 Elizabeth Allan published a book entitled *Burn on the Hill* (H2), based on his notebooks. Or at least some of them, for a number had been lost or destroyed and those that remain are only still in existence because a book collector came across and bought a bundle of ten at a London bookstall. Scrutiny, even to a non-walker, proved interesting, so he had an expert examine them, with the result that they are now held in the Archive Department of Aberdeen University's King's College Library. Gleaning information from his notebooks, Allan wrote an imaginative but accurate account of his journeys, capturing the atmosphere of a Gaelic-speaking community as he sat beside its firesides, recovering from his exertions and the hustle and bustle of travel necessary to reach the starting point of his labours. The whole affair is salutary reading for modern-day Munroists basking in their achievement of 280-odd mountains whilst leaning on the twin props of motorways and a detailed Ordnance Survey. What is more, an outcome of his activities was the start of a trend that gained increasing momentum, namely the long and continuous walk followed by a carefully noted account.

Many years later, two men were sitting in a Scottish bothy, its roof creaking in the night's wind.

'Have you ever thought about doing the Munros in one continuous go?'

The speaker was referring to Hamish Brown's circuit,

completed in 1974. The other considered the question and replied that if he were ever to consider such an enterprise he would probably choose the Corbetts instead.

'What about attempting them both?'

The query came from Craig Caldwell and for a year from February 1985 he did little else. The outcome of this monster stravaig of 498 tops was *Climb Every Mountain* (H40), published in 1990.

His friend's preferred choice of the Corbetts over the Munros is interesting. They were named after J Rooke Corbett, the fourth Munroist, who quickly realised that there were many fine hills under the magic 3,000 feet. British hill walkers would be all the poorer without Great Gable in the Lake District and Cader Idris in Wales. North of the border, they are spoiled for choice. Foinavon and Suilven in Sutherland, Ben Dearg in Torridon and Garbh Bheinn in Ardgour bear every comparison with loftier peaks and flag to the informed the existence of gems without the Tables. Then, moored off the coast, are the ridges of flagship Arran with its fleet of outriders straddling the Minch. Moreover, from Caldwell's point of view, as a collection, little had been written about them.

An obvious attraction is their nature. Possibly irritated by Munro's imprecision as to what constituted a mountain and what a top—or simply alarmed at the enormity facing a completion of every possible protuberance—Corbett adopted a straightforward formula. The summit must lie between the 3,000ft and 2,500ft contours and have a drop of 500 feet on all sides. Only those who, in thick mist, have attempted to distinguish the likes of Meall Dubhag and Carn Ban Mor from the surrounding uniformity can testify to the downside of Munro-bagging. This is particularly true when the eventual triumph of rendering the veil asunder is nullified by the SMC deciding, in its finite wisdom, to reduce them to the rank of mere tops. Collecting Corbetts is a more straightforward matter, as its strictures are more certain. Only resurveying can alter the firmament. The OS giveth and the OS taketh away.

Caldwell followed the ground rules laid down by Hamish Brown in his continuous journey around the Munros. With the exception of ferry travel to the Islands (mind you, a Menlove Edwards would have rowed across the Minch), the trip was to be self-propelled, either by bicycle or on foot. Caldwell also faced the same problems—planning the route around the stalking season while leaving relatively accessible hills for the inevitable winter months. As it would take at least the best part of a year to complete both sets, the second constriction loomed larger and, in the end, Caldwell decided on a March to March programme. This vaulting ambition nearly came unseated at an early stage. The final few feet of The Cobbler is an interesting and somewhat exposed scramble, which on

A Stroll in the Park

this occasion was covered with ice. Not carrying the requisite gear, he realised that an accident at this point would throw the whole expedition into disarray, so a tactical withdrawal and a redrawing of plans were deemed sensible.

Along with those of Hamish Brown (L8) and Martin Moran (H162), what the achievements of Burn and Caldwell had as their central objective was a pre-conceived target. This 'because it's there' approach has been, from Mallory to Munro, the common factor in most climbing activity and any subsequent literary account. The words evoking this desire might alter but it was essentially 'to knock the bastard off', the offending illegitimacy being the challenge that is currently staring you in the face. You don't climb Everest, the North Face of the Eiger or even all the Munros by chance. But, as these examples show, while it may be true that in some places the twin elements of summit and challenge might be one and the same thing, in the UK the pairing of the two is nearly always artificial. Either the difficulty is contrived by ignoring easier options or an arbitrary number of relatively simple challenges are lumped together into a collective difficulty.

One result of this was that complex, yet unwritten, rules and protocol had to be devised which decided that attaining the summit of Pillar Rock was more significant than the ascent of its parent mountain and, further to constrict this constriction, adjudged one slight variation in ascent more meritorious than another. It is little wonder that the activity falls easy prey to the satirist and in the consequent slanging match it was always likely that something important might be lost. If the tone of climbing literature was to become one of acerbic thrust and counter-thrust, the sublime immanence of the hills could be ignored when people came to write about the mountain experience. Terry Gifford in *Reconnecting with John Muir* describes the works of writers influenced by the Rock and Ice generation as inherently damaging. He argues that, while not wishing to return to a sentimentally romantic view of the hills, some forms of literary expression such as poetry—which, as much as climbing, is about exercising 'control under pressure'—might detrimentally be driven off the agenda.

Literature that related to walking might have fallen into its own, not dissimilar rut. The successors to Brown and Caldwell could have produced little more than guidebooks in disguise. But, in 1987, Dave Hewitt started a move in a new direction when he devised an expedition as much concerned with the revealing process as the triumphal product. Rather than collect a series of summits decreed by man, he would connect a series of summits concocted by nature. His decision was to walk the watershed of mainland Scotland. He had toyed with the idea of mainland Britain but the thought of irate English landowners and the perils of traversing Birmingham proved too off-putting, so he settled for a stravaig from Hobb's Flow on the English–Scottish border to Cape Wrath. Planning the route was relatively straightforward, as the shape of Scotland—unlike, say, Germany—creates a ribcage effect, with the rivers flowing off the watershed east and west into the North Sea or the Atlantic Ocean.

Such is the configuration of the hills that the watershed tends to the west and consequently crosses such delights as the Rough Bounds of Knoydart and the hills and hostel that encompass the Forest of Alladale. Inevitably, great chunks of the promised land are missing, notably Glencoe, the Cairngorms and the slender spires of Sutherland, but Hewitt concluded the defining lack of river crossing meant that he would have the compensating bonus of keeping his feet dry. Only at the top of the Reay Forest does the watershed split and force the traveller to decide on Cape Wrath or John o' Groats as the final destination. The imagined packs of Scottie dogs chewing shortbread while playing the bagpipes made the choice simple.

As it turned out, the route was anything but straightforward and as there was at least one watershed lochan that seemed to flow out of both ends, it would have been little short of miraculous if he had been able to keep his (foot)powder dry. In the event, this was a minor consideration, for it seemed most of the time spent on the hill was subject to wind and rain. In addition, Hewitt had estimated that the 80-day journey would be about 800 miles with 80,000 metres of ascent, a rather neat equation for a man who specialises in drawing up lists (the Tacit Tables) and endeavouring to discover whether it's possible to see all three Glasgow Underground illuminated U signs from one viewpoint. But life is not neat. It turned out to be over 850 miles with 100,000 metres of ascent. In 1994 his *magnus ambulus* was published as *Walking the Watershed* (H117).

Hewitt's walk appeared to mop up all that was left after Brown, Moran and Caldwell and there seemed little more to say about wild walking in the British Isles. But his journey had suggested an alternative approach. If John Muir was right when he implied that an account of a mountain walk should be more an understanding of man's relationship with his environment than a glorified tick list, then Hewitt's bowing to the dictates of the landscape was a step in that direction and Wainwright's *A Pennine Journey* had been ahead of its time. In a similar vein, Ronald Turnbull started to produce books on individual mountains. *The Riddle of Sphinx Rock* (H227) and *The Life and Times of the Black Pig* (H228) describe not only various routes to the summit of Great Gable and Ben Macdui respectively, but also add chapters on geology, history and legend to give a heightened sense of place.

Others followed. In 2008 Andrew Bibby published *The Backbone of England* (H20). Unlike his forerunners Wainwright and Tom Stephenson, he followed the true Pennine Watershed from Edale to Hadrian's Wall. Bibby was able to take advantage of the Countryside and Rights of Way Act that had opened up tracts of land on the Cumbrian–Durham border previously the preserve of those whose business and/or pleasure it was to shoot dodgy foreigners and low-flying birds. But this was much more than a record of the route followed and, in fact, is remarkably short of detail regarding footpaths and such difficulties as to which way gates open. Much of the description is taken up with the various encounters the author had with those—astronomers, shepherds, meteorologists, gamekeepers and the like—who live and work on the true backbone of the North.

Britain certainly has nothing approaching the sort of wilderness that inspired Muir, but it is essential for the survival of the planet that we understand the significance that the remoter parts of these islands still have in securing carbon sinks and important biological sanctuaries. Only those who walk the high land are aware of how matters are changing. And those who walk, then write about, the hills can make us all aware of that reality. Rather more successfully than those who clink their tungsten way to the local climbing wall.

His Story

There is no point in beating about the bush. 'Her story' just will not do. Nor will the politically correct 'His or Her Story', nor the more obviously obsequious 'Her or His Story'. As for the well-worn cop-out 'Their Story', I am afraid it simply doesn't make the cut. So, to mix Congreve with Shakespeare and deflect the severer excesses of whatever slings and arrows a Fury worse than Hell's can let loose, I had better explain. What follows is an assessment of recent biographical material and as it is a question of 'Whose life is it anyway?' I was rather taken by the fortuity of 'his story' and 'history'. I would gladly have used 'her story' and 'herstory' (*vide* slings and arrows *supra*) but the nearest I could recall was 'harstery', an 'archaic and soon defunct term for the feudal right to gather acorns during the winter months' which, even after careful consideration, didn't seem particularly relevant.

Moreover, with the exception of Jan Levi's life of Muriel Barker (H137), the female contribution to recent climbing biographies of the requisite type appears somewhat thin on the ground. Not that such absence of record is unusual or confined to the female sex. There are great chunks of British climbing history where we know little about the great and the good, other than their achievements on rock and snow. There is not much about Raeburn, Archer Thomson or the Abraham brothers. Of Botterill and Samson before the war, or Kelly and Holland in its immediate aftermath, there is scarcely a word. Perhaps the slaughter put matters in a different perspective. Perhaps it was felt that the climbs sufficiently revealed the man. Whatever the reason, I am left with what is available and, as I have neither the guile of Penelope nor the creative skills of Scheherazade to spin a tale out of one book, I have chosen to make do with an all-male contribution.

But an absence of detailed information does not stop the curiosity of others. In fact, it tends to provoke it. If you are climbing up, failing on or falling off the likes of Oliverson's *Variation*, Abrahams' *New* West or even Popplethwaite's *Alternative Indirect Finish*, you might well wonder what prompted these subversions of the norm, what momentous decisions were reached before stepping into the unknown. Indeed, what sort of men were the perpetrators of such unorthodoxy. It was not until I came across an entry in a Tryfan guide describing a short chimney route on Drws Nodded that I began to understand. One hundred feet long (or short), it had crept into the lowly grade of Just Difficult, a title bestowed, no doubt, to soften the accompanying blow of 'not a good climb, the bottom half being only a few feet from easy ground'. If the guidebook writer had been in a more perceptive mood, he might in his historical introduction have paused to acknowledge this particular moment. The instant when one A G N Flew, freed from his travails in the laboratory, had on 26th September 1948 at last found his Holy Grail, a route up a chimney that was not only within his capabilities but, more importantly, had avoided the attention of the early pioneers. A route which, triumphantly, he could christen Analyst's Flue. It doesn't quite have the ring of Jones' Route Direct from Lord's Rake or Master's Wall but, nevertheless, it must have afforded its own sense of satisfaction.

Perhaps that is the real reason for biography. A pandering to the reader's demand to know the inside story. In a way, the matter is not dissimilar to name-dropping, a chance to cosy up to the famous. You may never have climbed Cemetery Gates on the Cromlech nor met either Brown or Whillans but, in the comfort of your armchair, you know the full story. That, as they made the journey back to Manchester trying to think of a name for their new route, they spotted a bus bearing the legend that fitted both the nature of the climb and the nomenclature of its neighbours. For a second or two you might have been riding pillion yourself that September night in 1951, an honorary member of the Rock and Ice. There is a sense of the archaeological dig in finding out what actually happened, and why it did. But before embarking on such a task it might be wise for the burrower to remember that the step between digging for history and robbing a grave is not that great.

A social consequence of the Second World War was that more people took to climbing, and more climbers meant the emergence of new stars who pushed back the previously accepted frontiers. Eventually these innovators grew old and the most successful, or more literate, decided to cash in. This biographical outcome might be collectively entitled *Air on a Clothes Line*.

As a result, there was a danger that a formula might become too well-established, with its own version of the Seven Ages of Man: the 'Human Fly' (1) tells of early beginnings with make-do equipment; (2) meets Great Man who explains mysteries of hand-jamming; (3) solves all Last Great Problems with suitable bemusement at all the fuss; (4) transfers hand-jamming expertise to Alps/Yosemite/Acapulco; (5) attains mythic status by saying nothing and adopting an enigmatic smile (with or without carefully angled fag); (6) perfects the 'snow-jam' (aka Dead Man's Handshake) on the North East Face of Kanga Chobbliwobbly before finally (7) hinting at his particular exit strategy chosen from (a) exploiting commercial possibilities by promoting climbing gear and lucrative *après-roche* wear; (b) opening chain of shops to sell same; (c) avoiding any real climbing by organising others to do the hard bits before cashing in on book sales, or (d) quietly fading away to become a merchant banker.

Fortunately this has not been the case. The climber's mythic status seemed to have lost its grip. The early television excitement surrounding the sea stacks off the Scottish coast and atmospheric cliff climbing on Anglesey faded away with the scramble for cast-off gear and BBC expense accounts. A name was no longer enough, the author must have something worth saying, or at least cast his line in a different direction. Ed Drummond's *A Dream of White Horses* (H78) is certainly not formulaic. It contains a variety of genre, and amongst the poems and essays there is a review of Perrin's *Menlove* (H174). Drummond praises the author for his particular approach in that he describes climbers as people, rather than people as climbers. It could, he suggests 'knock [mountaineering] off its pedestal'.

Later developments suggest that Drummond might well have been right. In 2005, Andy Cave was awarded the Boardman Tasker Prize for his autobiography *Learning to Breathe* (H45). This tells the story of a young man who lived and worked through the Miners' Strike of the Eighties. Apart from some of the difficulties that filtered through the more sympathetic parts of the press, the public had little idea of what was really happening in these pit villages, or that in the long term an irreplaceable social fabric was being destroyed. Life surrounded the pit head, which produced tight-knit communities that offered a level of support and social harmony that had long been the staple of rural England. Now, torn between political outrage and economic need, families and friends were rent apart as some remained on strike while others crossed the picket line. People were forced to move away from areas where their family had lived for generations, son inheriting father's job.

For most, there was no way out of this debilitating depression. Andy Cave was lucky. He had climbing. From the early beginnings of scrabbling up the pit muckstack as a child, then climbing on the local gritstone edges, he followed the usual progression through British rock and winter climbing on to the Alps. In 1986, one year after the strike came to an end, he abandoned his job, became a full-time mountaineer and started from scratch to gain a PhD in sociolinguistics. In *Learning to Breathe* there are echoes of the Mass Trespasses of the Thirties and the great tram escape from both sides of the Pennines into the Peak District, but in this case freed from the romantic window-dressing that history can so artfully arrange.

One story sums up the whole affair. Cave and a friend would, under cover of darkness, partly to keep fit, partly out of the devilment born of boredom, climb the various buildings they came across in Sheffield. On one occasion they were caught climbing up the side of a doctor's house. The police understandably thought they were burglars, a suspicion compounded when Cave admitted he worked at Grimethorpe, renowned as one of the most militant collieries in Yorkshire. The police don't rush investigations of this sort, allowing the suspect to spend a cold and unpleasant night in the cell. Forensic evidence soon showed that Cave had not climbed the drainpipe, the obvious method of entry, but via an apparently holdless wall. Yet it was not until the afternoon of the next day that he was released. It was not long after this that Cave realised it was time to get out. The chapter is entitled 'Into the Light'.

The interrelation between the work of the miner and his play lies more deeply embedded than in most occupations. Anyone who has not visited a pit face when it is in full operation has little idea of the conditions. The relevant section from George Orwell's *Road to Wigan Pier* gives, as far as any second-hand experience can, a good idea of the difficulties and should be required reading for anyone thinking of going into politics. Working conditions have improved since Orwell described his visit underground but the heat and dust are the same. Miners are issued dust-masks but, at times, the conditions make them intolerable to wear and the machinery provided to ease the sheer intensity of manual labour carries its own dangers of miscalculation and mangled limbs. The collapsing roof and inexplicable explosion are ever present.

One of the most compelling accounts in this climbing biography is not about climbing at all. Yet, paradoxically, it is the climber who is probably the best outsider to have any understanding of what it really involved. As was often the case, the gang were in a hurry to get to the pit bottom to catch the early cage. To save time, they decided to ride the coal conveyor belt, a practice that was both forbidden and highly dangerous. Although it was only travelling at ten miles an hour, the pitch black and the constriction of the tunnel made it feel as though you were travelling at ten times that speed. You had to leap onto this moving snake of coal and hope that some sudden shift in the roof had not altered the shape of the tunnel, producing an unforeseen obstruction which might result in decapitation. The real problem was getting off. As you were in a prone position, you would have to lurch to the left, grabbing a waterpipe, then, in virtually the same movement, swing your legs clear. All this had to be done as quickly as possible to avoid detection or ending up in the cogs of the belt engine.

Only those used to taking potentially fatal risks and being the butt of gallows humour embroidered by old hands to impress callow youth, can hope to appreciate that heart-stopping moment as the leap is made. There are, as you would expect in a book on mountaineering, many similar accounts of decisions taken and outcomes uncertain. None more so than during the terrifying descent of Changabang in the Himalayas. But the one aspect that distinguishes this book from others dealing with climbs at home and abroad is that it forms a fitting literary climax to the story of a significant social change. The years when the interlacing of the hardships of industrial labour and the discovery of the freedom of the hills meant men collectively and individually learnt to breathe.

Another book that lies off the beaten track is *Vertical Pleasure: The Secret Life of a Taxman* (H88). Even if you don't assume it is out of the same byre as *Confessions of a Window Cleaner*, you would regard the explanatory part of the title as a contradiction in terms. Taxmen simply don't have secret lives: no Clark Kent/Superman routine lies behind the faceless features of the perpetrators of over-complicated forms. The kindest thing you can say of the taxman is that he is reliable. The sort of man who fits the well-worn phrase 'what you see is what you get' like a sensibly designed glove.

Cue Mick Fowler. He is a taxman and, as Assistant Director of Capital Taxes, a taxman of some standing. He is also a climber. One whom Chris Bonington described as 'the most successful innovative mountaineer of the last twenty years'. He was awarded, with his partner Paul Ramsden, the Piolet D'or—probably the greatest accolade in climbing—for their ascent of the North Face of Siguniang, a remote mountain in China. His local CV is equally impressive. New routes in this country range from the Outer Hebrides to Gogarth (he specialises in sea stacks), one of the first E6 routes in the Peak District and several Grade VI ice climbs in Scotland. Abroad, his air-mile tally includes trips to

Peru, Nepal, Pakistan, India and China. However, the most remarkable thing is that he does all this during his annual leave. Not for him the begging round of gear manufacturers or chasing after a place on some polynational expedition. He simply packs his sack, buys his plane ticket and sets off on his holidays.

The above are autobiographies and therefore, prima facie, tell the story as its subject wants it to be heard. But there is also the alternative of others delving into history and telling the tale of those unwilling or unable to tell it for themselves. The life stories of Siegfried Herford (H224), Colin Kirkus (H74) and Jock Nimlin (H220) have all surfaced, thanks to the existence and support of such small independent publishers as The Ernest Press.

But the mountain biography that was sufficiently popular to be reprinted in paperback was not of a man who pioneered new ground-breaking routes on vertical rock but of one who was so concerned about leaving terra firma that he would go miles out of his way to find an unlocked gate rather than climb over some conveniently placed wall.

Hunter Davies' sympathetic account of the life and times of Alfred Wainwright (H72) is now well known. Part One: the ill-tempered alcoholic father, the struggle to reach the first rungs of the white-collar ladder, and the unsuccessful marriage, when Ruth Holden, not surprisingly, failed to measure up to AW's emotional hopes of his 'Dream Girl'. Part Two: the counterbalancing move to Kendal, where many of his frustrations were sublimated by his 'new love', founded on a full exploration of the Lake District, and how, a recluse in his own house, he wrote, then published his *Pictorial Guides*. Part Three: the appearance of his 'Dream Girl' in the form of Betty McNally, financial success from his writings, which in turn enabled significant financial support for the development of the Cumbria Animal Rescue Centre. (All this, in the hands of a certain type of film producer, to be made into a drama in three acts—young man embittered through frustration eventually makes good, supported by loyal animal-loving second wife, with a final reverse zoom fade of the former old curmudgeon overlooking his beloved Lakeland, cradling an injured lamb.)

My Thesaurus does not contain the word to describe the spinning that would take place up on Haystacks if such a thing were to occur. As it happens, the centenary of Wainwright's birth revitalised his reputation and his ghost must have allowed himself half a smile at the thought of television still clutching him to its bosom long after it had discarded the photogenic opportunities of the 'Human Fly'.

There is a third type of 'his story' and that is where a second biographer revisits the biography or autobiography of another. This might happen for a variety of reasons, the most obvious being the discovery of, or access to, new material. Another is to look at the existing evidence in a new light. Jim Perrin's biographies of Menlove Edwards and Don Whillans are a mixture of both.

There is an excellent example in *Menlove. The Life of John Menlove Edwards* (H174). From a reading of *Samson: the Life and Writings of Menlove Edwards* by Geoffrey Sutton and Wilfred Noyce (L42), written some twenty odd years earlier, you would be aware that Edwards was a homosexual and that much of the trauma of his life lay in trying to come to terms with this in both a general and specific way. But such were the circumstances, the criminality of the act and the identification of the individuals involved, that matters were left understandably blurred. The passing of time allowed Perrin to illuminate this deliberate twilight and produce a book that would 'vindicate his subject'. A simple way to do this was by an example that shows rather than says. In this case, an example too painful to be recalled in *Samson*.

Over one Christmas period, Edwards was staying with Noyce and other guests at the home of Professor Pigou. Gatesgarth was a stone mansion surrounded by woods; billiards and a private beach were available for any party Pigou chose to collect. Noyce regarded Pigou as his 'fairy godfather' (amongst other things he picked up the tab for Noyce's visits to the Alps) and as New Year's Eve was Noyce's birthday, each of the guests gave him a present. The host went first and produced a top of the range Leica camera with all the accompanying bells and whistles. It came to Edwards' turn. His present was also a Leica camera but the most basic of models. The poignancy of the moment needs no explanation. It must have been clear to Edwards, faced with this accumulation of wealth and social standing, that if the head of Noyce was to be turned, it would not, in the long term, be in Menlove's direction.

After Edwards, Perrin decided to try another complicated climber. There had already been published a book on Don Whillans. This *Portrait of a Mountaineer* (L43), published in 1971, was a collaboration between the climber and Alick Ormerod and as such is both autobiography and biography. The structure is quite interesting. Whillans gives the impression of telling his own story but it is probable that Ormerod's role was to give it some sort of cohesive pattern. Whillans would remember the bombing in the Second World War and Ormerod would add the historical circumstances. Whillans recalls his first climb with Joe Brown, Ormerod adds the 'human interest' detail, plus a thumbnail sketch of Brown as a renowned rock climber. The twin narrators are distinguished by Ormerod's direct contribution appearing in italics. I say 'direct', as there are signs that Whillans' testimony has been tailored to fit into the overall plan and here, unitalicised, the hand of the professional must indirectly lie.

The problem for the reader is how to tell who decided to omit or include what, and the basis of Perrin's rebiography *The Villain* (H179) seems to be to examine and, if possible, elucidate what really happened. Of his sister, mother and father, Whillans has little or nothing to say, leaving such biographic detail as was necessary to Ormerod. More surprisingly, his wife Audrey receives the same treatment. You might have thought that there would have been some word of thanks for the woman who financially and selflessly made it possible for him to devote his life to climbing.

Perrin's investigation throws some light on this. Whillans' behaviour towards his wife was boorish at best. An example of his attitude towards her was recalled by Leo Dickinson, where Audrey, having been at work all day, returned home and immediately made the pair of them a cup of tea. Whillans spat out the first mouthful and roundly berated her for not stirring it first. If this was typical of his behaviour towards her in general, it is not surprising that he shows so little literary appreciation of the part she played in his success. Ormerod's contribution is that she had seemed to Whillans 'to possess all the attributes necessary to make a climber's girl'.

Perrin mentions Audrey rather more. Each occasion is equally depressing. He recounts examples of her being taken for granted, brought along to the Alps to do the cooking, belittled in front of others Whillans, presumably, wished to impress and being subjected to outbursts of jealousy, such as the Keswick 'dob of dobs', when a tourist made the mistake of wolf-whistling at her. On such matters neither Whillans nor Ormerod have very much to say.

And that is not surprising. The absence of negative detail can be axiomatic of an autobiography, particularly if written by someone as egocentric as Whillans. In his account of the ascent of the Bonatti Pillar he places himself firmly centre stage, not entirely without justice in view of the expedition's various disasters. Three parties had joined as one and the combined mishaps of its members contributed to Whillans' view that he had become embroiled with a 'troupe of acrobats'. From the general shambles, he singled out his climbing partner, Paul Ross, for particular scorn. Perrin, however, has heard Ross's side of the story and reveals that there was already ill-feeling between the pair. This centred around Whillans' inappropriate approaches to Ross's girlfriend and his failure to climb Ross's *pièce de résistance*, Post Mortem on Eagle Crag. It seems that Ross felt Whillans had got the Bonatti Pillar affair out of proportion and was happy to reveal that, when it came to the descent of the mountain, rather than an orderly retreat with Whillans as self-professed benevolent ringmaster, it was a case of every man for himself.

This might have been little more than pots and kettles, but a more significant difference between the two books concerns Whillans' relationship with Joe Brown. If you read the autobiography, you get the impression that the pair started to climb together more or less by chance and the partnership flourished because Whillans was the only person able to match Brown's ambition.

Perrin has a rather different story. Joe Dutton, who knew both men well, believed that Whillans actively courted Brown, visiting his house and monopolising his conversation as though trying to establish the Brown–Whillans team as a cut above the rest of the Rock and Ice. Matters went well between them until Brown was invited to the Himalayas. Dutton actually uses the term 'jilted' to describe Whillans' reaction— and Don had always been possessive of Joe, being aggressively rude to any girlfriend as though fearful that marriage would terminate their relationship. When Brown eventually did marry, Whillans, according to Don Roscoe, actively hated Valerie, blaming her for taking Joe from him. He also appeared to be envious of Brown's success. It was Brown who was invited on the prestigious expeditions, became the star of television and was courted by the media.

On the other hand, in the autobiography, Whillans gives the impression to Ormerod that matters just came to an end and that Brown had just become 'part of the past'. No reason given and apparently none asked for.

But does this mean that Whillans and Ormerod were being economical with the truth, whereas Perrin is revealing the actuality? Many of these differences could be put down to shades of opinion, but there is one incident which seems to revolve around matters of fact. It concerns the first ascent of Taurus on the Pinnacle Face of Clogwyn du'r Arddu, which Whillans led after Brown had failed. From the autobiographer, there is not a word about this impressive lead and his Boswell lumps the ascent together with the Girdle Traverse of Dinas Cromlech and Sceptre. Therefore the impression the reader gets is that the route was of little particular consequence to Whillans and only included by Ormerod for the historical reason that it was Whillans' last new route on Cloggy.

Perrin's version has more to tell, both about the climb and the climbers. Brown was debilitated after his recent trip to Kanchenjunga and, climbing in vibrams for the first time on British rock, had already struggled on the relatively easy Sunset Crack. Then, thoroughly unnerved by the presence of a loose block, he backed off the new route. Whillans climbed to the block, gave it a good thump and proceeded to use it as a runner. With little more to-do, he completed the climb. Not surprisingly, as Taurus was graded XS while Sunset Crack was a mild-mannered VS, Brown struggled and called for a tight rope. Nothing happened. Further appeals were also ignored, leaving Brown no option but to haul himself up by any parts of his anatomy available. Don's comment when Joe finally floundered onto the belay was, 'I reckon this will go down as *my* Cenotaph Corner.'

As the detail is very similar, Perrin presumably used the account in Brown's autobiography *The Hard Years* (L9) as his source. There is, however, one subtle difference. According to Perrin, Whillans 'leered' as he made his deflatory remark, suggesting a certain level of vindictiveness that Perrin believed was consistent with his behaviour elsewhere. Brown, on the other hand, considered it was meant as a tease, albeit at that moment the joke was wearing rather thin. Where does the truth lie? Is Whillans' absence of comment in his autobiography a sign of remorse or disdain? Is Perrin inventing an emotional reaction that did not exist? Did the vindictiveness pass over Brown's head?

One final bit of confusion shows how difficult it is to pin down the past. The completion of Taurus took place not in 1956 as Ormerod states but in 1955 and, chronologically flanked by Slanting Slab and Woubits, was the centrepiece of Whillans' very hard trio of climbs that summer. This means that Taurus was not his last climb on Cloggy and was done after Brown returned from Kanchenjunga and not, as Ormerod suggests, before he left for the Karakoram. Was this careless research or did he, either under instruction or off his own bat, decide to sweep the event under the carpet with a couple of unconnected routes?

Even with all this information to hand, there is a sense that the reader is no further forward. Wherever the truth lies, it will never lie precisely in the assumption of a man's motives from what he does or says. When you know someone, it is difficult to be dispassionate and Perrin began to regard his book as a 'poisoned chalice'. Eventually, he just gathered the testimonies available, offering them without explicit comment, then issuing the disclaimer that 'in a sense, this book has been written not by [him], but by the community of British climbers'. By the time Perrin was invited to discuss *The Villain* at Leeds International Festival of Mountaineering Literature, his demeanour suggested he felt he may have made a mistake in undertaking the project at all and, rather than launching into any graphic detail on his subject, he chose to read from his coda on Chew Piece, a quiet reflective passage that seemed to sum up his feelings.

Perhaps it would have been better to let the myth stand. It was what Whillans wanted to believe as his story. It was what his admirers wanted to believe as history: a tough nut who dobbed men twice his size, did climbs that no one could follow and was thought by the best of his contemporaries to be a climber in whom you could put the utmost trust to get you out of anything, anywhere. Maybe that lack of 'herstory' has more to it than meets the eye.

Smoke and Mirrors

Historically, there are three types of climbing fiction: (1) Sensational: *Slowly her once carefully manicured fingernails slipped off the edge of the precipitous cliff.* (Ed. Don't be alarmed, there's a jolly strong chap swaddled in rope about to enter stage left); (2) as background and local colour for a particular genre of fiction: for example, the whodunit, *Death on Milestone Buttress* (Glyn Carr), or the historical novel, *Hazard's Way* (H121); and (3) the last and most important from a literary point of view, the novel or short story where the climbing intrinsically contributes to the development and understanding of character, while mirroring the social issues of its time. In that field *One Green Bottle* by Elizabeth Coxhead (L13) had stood, if not alone, at least at the head of a very short queue. Despite the shortfall, I believe that fiction of this type is the best direction left for new and different books dealing with the cliffs and hills of Britain.

Originally, the bulk of published books about climbing had ranged between memoir doubling as guidebook or instructional manual, and a solemn or humorous investigation into the nature of climbers and climbing. O G Jones (L22) and the Abraham brothers (L1/L2) had tended towards the former approach, while the likes of R B Frere (L15) and Alastair

Borthwick (L7) had favoured the latter. Once the sport had become sufficiently established, biographies of the great and good appeared and, though they continue to do so, their emphasis is moving away from British climbing. The eyes of today's climber turn outwards and now such books, after a chapter or two acknowledging the advantage of an apprenticeship on local rock and ice, concentrate on the greater ranges beyond.

Examples of the established genres (1) and (2) continue to appear, particularly the whodunit with its predictably predictable format. After all, there is a limit to the number of ways Miss Marple can solve the crime and the writer can conceal the murderer. *Murder in the Glen* by Hamish MacInnes (H144) gives a twist by introducing a real poacher-turned-gamekeeper to outwit the local PC MacPlod, and the author uses his intimate knowledge of the Glencoe area and mountain rescue expertise to good effect. Moreover, although the format is familiar, the *modus operandi* of the villain is cleverly enough contrived to keep the reader guessing. Nevertheless, the climbing whodunit is beginning to be more of the same. Time, perhaps, for a climbing whodunwot?

One interesting variant on the mountain book that draws on historical reality is a taut, well-written thriller, *The Return of John Macnab* by Andrew Greig (H106). Published in 1996, it is a reprise of a 1925 John Buchan novel where three distinguished middle-aged men, bored with the apparent ease of their lives, risk their reputations by poaching game in the Highlands. The owners of the estates are given due notice of where and when these criminal acts will take place and told to do their damnedest. There are sub-plots of romance and political elections to keep the main plot boiling as the drama unfolds. The late 20th-century version essentially follows the same lines, with Kirsty Fowler added as a d'Artagnan to these particular three musketeers. Mountaineering takes a greater part than in the original, with copies of Munro Tables, unclimbed rock and climbers' jargon strewn through the story, and the debate on land ownership moves from the relative merits of old and new money to the question of access for all and the implications of a Criminal Justice Act that attempts to empower the owners.

In this essay, however, I want to concentrate on the sort of recent fiction that uses climbing inherently to develop character or plot, rather than the type that uses it as a backdrop of swirling mists and potential peril to heighten suspense or concoct a denouement. An excellent past example of the sort of thing that I am looking for is the above-mentioned Coxhead novel, where the climbing, from Cathy's petulant failure on The Ordinary Route on the Slabs to her triumph of a long, unprotected lead on Cloggy, parallels a developing understanding of herself and those around her, while investigating the various worlds it might be possible for her to inhabit. But this was written more than fifty years ago and deals with the issues of that time. The question is, has anything followed that is more relevant to today's reader?

At first sight, *Todhra* (H102) by Dennis Gray seems to fit the bill as a serious climbing novel. The subject, the place of the gay male in the macho world of sport, is certainly relevant, as in most sporting activities a variety of prejudice has been deeply embedded. Footballers have been adjudged homosexual by fellow players, and sections of the crowd, on such tenuous ground as they bought and read *The Guardian*. There is no doubt that *Todhra* is a novel about climbing. The protagonist is a leading exponent and the reader is taken on a grand tour of the climbing scene from bouldering in Paris to a new attempt on Nanga Parbat. British climbing interest is well served, with accounts on Yorkshire outcrops, Welsh slate quarries and the north face of the Ben, as well as snapshots of local climbers on the walls of Mile End and the Grand Prix championship at Leeds.

All the basic ingredients are there, but what proof does the pudding offer? About half way through, digesting the detail becomes more difficult. So far in the book, which was published in 2005, there has been no indication that the events described are taking place at any time other than in the recent past, with the novel acting as a comment on current attitudes. But if that is the case, the story appears anachronistic. It seems very unlikely that in the 21st century the described behaviour of a certain part of the audience at an International Climbing Grand Prix would be tolerated, let alone it should use such outdated rhyming slang as 'ginger beer' for 'queer'. It is even more unlikely that a group of fellow climbers would be so concertedly affronted by John's sexual predilection as to be reduced to the behaviour of the worst sort of football supporter. Moreover, would Duncan, who otherwise appears as a kindly and concerned friend and mentor, be so horrified when he learns what he assumes is the truth as to immediately sever the relationship? The reader's reaction to this last revelation is particularly important if the book is to be considered a successful climbing novel in the terms I've suggested. At some point, or points, climbing and the central theme have to come together, each illuminating the other. If the reader has had difficulty in accepting the validity of either, the pudding, as it were, might stick in the gullet.

The dodgy silver thruppenny bit finally emerges when, towards the end of the book, there is a specific reference to Boycott as a potential captain of Yorkshire. As this cricketing furore occurred in the late Seventies, we now realise we were under a misapprehension and that the events described were taking place thirty years ago. The author is not writing about the problems of the homosexual climber today, but about a climbing age when homophobia was generally

rife. There is nothing wrong with deliberately misleading the reader, provided the deception is a device to
achieve some literary end. Nor is there anything amiss
with revisiting the past. But if an old story is to have
the worth of contemporary relevance, it needs to offer
something more than a retelling of history with the
names changed. The majority of the characters, and
especially the protagonist, must engage our interest
and the unfolding of events must seem credible when
viewed from another age.

Todhra does not help itself on any of these counts.
The confusion seems more accidental than deliberate. The novel fails to engage the reader with a fresh
take on an old subject and, with the exception of the
protagonist, the characters tend towards caricature.
Though there is no doubting the nature of the leading
man, it's difficult to sympathise with his lot. John is
self-centred from beginning to end and much given to
self pity. As he has been dealt a hand in life that means
that ultimately he cannot lose, unlike Coxhead's hero-
ine he seems to learn little on his journey, except that
it is unwise to practise unprotected sex with strangers
or to allow yourself to be drugged by lascivious Arabs.

For many people, the strength of the book will lie
in the accuracy with which the author describes the
range of climbing available to those prepared to treat
the sport as a lifestyle rather than a recreation, and
you cannot but be impressed by the way Gray brings

the climbs and climbing to life. These almost separate passages demonstrate the sureness of touch and accuracy of detail to be found in *Rope Boy* (L16), his 1970 autobiographical classic. In fact, if *Todhra* had been published nearer that time, it might have had similar success but today it seems to offer too little too late. As one reviewer put it: 'I suspect the book had a lengthy gestation' but, more tellingly, he also added that he, as a critic, may well have been 'preoccupied by the responsibility of being a heterosexual reader of a gay book'. Of course, my carping would be completely irrelevant if the novel was never meant to be anything more than a nostalgic sex 'n' shopping story, with its own version of the Mile High Club.

So if, as would appear, the selection of a controversial subject does not automatically provide a rewarding read, then what does work? As I've said, it seems to me that the author must by some means engage the interest of the reader in the issues under discussion and make the characters, however far-fetched, ring true. Moreover, if it is to be a good 'climbing' read, the events described must appear realistic to a mountaineer. M John Harrison's *Climbers* (H115) scores highly on both counts.

There are many specific moments that show that this book is about climbing. None more striking than those descriptions that all climbers would recognise as belonging to their pastime: the panicking clatter of gear when things go awry, the hasty stuffing of the sack as the weather turns, wandering around gear shops like women in fashion stores, the desire for ticks on the wish list, the obsession with doing a climb properly, the preponderance of teachers. On one occasion, one of the characters completes what he thinks is a new climb which he wants to christen Peanut Power, only to discover that it's already been done and named Masters of the Modern Dance—*The fucking wimps.*

Moreover, a serious novel must have substance and *Climbers* certainly has that. Published in 1989, it casts a jaundiced eye on the results of Thatcher's Britain and reflects the views of those who, through either taste or inclination, felt uneasy with a regime that valued the regulation of teachers and doctors above restricting the potential excesses of short-sellers and manipulators of hedge funds. But it is far from being a rant. The narrative unfolds in the hands of Mike, whose first-person viewpoint and apparently dispassionate reportage allow the author to make comment and judgement without continually nudging the reader in the ribs.

The account, for there is really no story, is of a loose-knit group of youngish and not so youngish men who wash between the shores of friend- and acquaintance-ship: Mike, the narrator, Normal, his mentor, Bob Almanac, a teacher, and Sankey, who had once been 'the finest climber in the valley'. Youth, in the form of Gaz, Mick and Stox, from time to time puts the boot in. Women are there, yet not there. Living in and around the foot of the Pennines, and both rejecting and rejected by the society that surrounds them, this group of men channel their energy, together with their hopes and fears, into climbing.

In practice, they have no grand design. North Wales maybe, but mostly they are content to burrow around in the disused quarries or windswept gritstone edges of northern England. The one concession to ambitious grandeur is Normal's ongoing plan to complete a rock garden which is to contain a sample from every major cliff in Britain, with a chunk of Cloggy as the centrepiece. Otherwise, there are only dreams. Dreams of a soaring unending crack riven in warm, off-vertical rock with perfect holds and, at perfectly placed intervals, 'terrific foot-jams' to allow the dreamer a contented rest. Other dreams are more frightening, where the crack suddenly clamps shut like a jaw, with the climber unable to move either up or down.

Ostensibly, this account is trapped in the framework of the four seasons, yet, as if to escape, spills back and forth in time. For some, the past is perpetually present. At Sankey's funeral, Normal is excited by a glimpse of former famous names he can add to his historic memorabilia. Bob Almanac loosens an old knot in a time-tired rope to release the colours trapped inside. For others, there are dreams of future cars and climbs and, until the Falkland War intervened, expeditions to

South America in search of mythical creatures. And so the novel develops through the unrelenting cycles against a shifting background of mist and sodden rock. The climbers, obsessively, slide into their own world, the 'real' world assuming for them the 'fake-surrealist air of a cigarette advert'.

In the opening chapter there are two episodes pivotal to an understanding of the novel. In the first, Normal is at great pains to take the narrator to a point 'abandoned to the steaming mist' in the commercial and municipal no man's land of a grouse moor on the border of Yorkshire and Greater Manchester. The view he wants Mike to see, and the camera to record, is a quarry that has been turned into a rubbish dump, crowned with a sodden, moquette three-piece suite and festooned with grown-out-of children's clothing and pages torn from pornographic magazines. Like Wilfred Owen before him, who sent his images of truth to Parliament, Normal sends his photographs of protest to climbing magazines, perhaps hoping they might kick-start some sort of crusade. Inevitably, in this annexe of Disneyland, they are rejected in favour of the rippling muscles of famous names poised on sun-strewn rock. From the start, the satirical nail is given a pretty firm whack.

In the second episode, the narrator recalls sitting, as a child, in a brightly illuminated cafe surrounded by plastic tables and chairs and hovering waitresses. A mirror image is reflected in the tinted plate-glass window, so that it seems there is another, identical cafe in the rain-swept car park where the same waitresses paddle through puddles and lay their trays on the polished bonnets of patiently waiting cars. A looking-glass world in a world where wealth creates waste. A world of smoke and mirrors.

But the real challenge for the author lies in inter-weaving these abstract ideas into the actual descrip-tions of the book's principal activity. Harrison tackles this element with such care and quiet precision that a casual reading can easily miss the point. There is an early example when Normal is trying to clean up a route on a nondescript crag one bitter winter's day. He 'is stalled out halfway up the cliff'. The choice of the verb 'stalled' is effective. Both the emotional and phys-ical engines have cut out and left the individual poised in frustrated impotence, that combination of physical and mental paralysis that every climber, at one time or another, must have experienced.

This early image seeps into the book as it charts the course of the various characters while they try to make sense of a life that circumstance has thrust upon them. Characters abandon jobs that seem pointless, only to discover that the alternative is no more fulfilling. Mick gives up his floor-sweeping, where he at least gets some satisfaction when he is allowed to smash up faulty piping, for a job as a National Park Warden with an official National Park Land Rover, which in actuality entails clearing up the traditional debris from scenic car parks.

It is later given a more concrete form in an overheard conversation concerning a little boy who covered his soft toys in sticking plasters before immuring them between the panes of a double-glazed window. Closer re-examination of the earlier passage shows the immediate relevance of this to Normal's frustrated efforts. His effort *is* stalled, rather than *has* stalled. The choice of 'is' over 'has' appears to make little difference—in fact I recalled the quote incorrectly when I was making some notes for this essay—but further thought shows how important it is. If the choice of auxiliary verb had lain between 'Normal *has* eaten' and 'Normal *is* eaten', the difference would have been obvious, yet the distinction here is equally important. Normal *has* not stalled in the sense that he is temporally resting before refiring the starter. He *is* stuck, as in a trap, unable to make any further meaningful progress, another wounded teddy bear corralled in a chosen form of aspic.

I would be straining at a gnat if the description of Normal stuck on a cliff was a lone example of the employment of metaphor to illustrate meaning, but images tumble out of the text. Almost every anecdote has another layer that connects with the ideas of the book at large. To take one other example, Mike first discovers the satisfaction that can be gained from solving climbing problems when he has to escape from an 'area' that encloses a cellar window. He has jumped into it to rescue a supposedly trapped cat, only to find himself stuck. There is a great to-do as a gathering crowd offers a confusion of suggestions and helping hands. The cat, of course, scrabbles up the wall in its own time and saunters off unperturbed. Mike eventually works out the necessary dynamics and, through a combination of balance and body position, hauls himself unaided out of the well.

There is a further character, unannounced but often present. Through the cyclic movement of the seasons and the shifting images of time, there is the continual click of the camera as it ranges over Harrison's Waste Land. An old fading photograph has recorded Normal's dilemma. Sankey stands below, his cagoule billowing in the wind, as if trying to fly to the rescue. The camera, a reliable if unsympathetic witness, another Tiresias, sees it all, the huddle of fish-out-of-water mourners at Sankey's funeral, the sodden three-piece suite, the tattily glamorised naked bodies, revealing what is really there, rather than the hyped-up, hoped-for version.

There has, however, to be more to an important novel than a few literary flourishes. It should examine some area from a fresh perspective, and the good and indeed great novels intersplice an account of character and events with some dominant and usually signifi-cant theme or themes. At one stage in the novel, Bob

Almanac suggests that climbing is a form of 'escapology'. By that he does not mean the false avoidance of risk as in 'escapism', but that climbers, like Houdini, unnecessarily place themselves in a position of danger to experience the ecstasy of triumph and relief that success might bring. On an earlier occasion, the narrator mulls over the phrase 'the pornography of risk', as performed by fit young men and women clad in striped lycra, a phrase that he has heard, but is unsure as to what it means, or if it means anything at all.

The author appears to lay side by side these two perspectives of what climbing might be all about, then leave you to it. There are prompts, however, which suggest possible connections between these enigmatic comments. After Sankey's sudden death while climbing, Mick discovers a stash of girlie-mags which he rather shamefacedly buries in one of their former owner's half-finished building projects. We eventually discover Normal's real motive for visiting the second-hand bookshop was not in the professed hope of finding some lost mountaineering gem, but to examine the section containing the more profitable books for sale, in the hopes of spicing up his marriage. These sideways glances in the mirror allow a shadowy apparition to appear—one of dissatisfied striving against a mixture of tacky advertising, unbridled greed and a certain type of populist politics—and hover in the smoke of the reader's mind.

Although this is little more than a surface analysis of the areas the book covers and the way it covers them, its purpose is to suggest that a closer reading and re-reading can pay dividends. When *Climbers* was submitted for the Boardman Tasker Prize, there was much discussion, often negative, as to its 'suitability'. Jim Perrin cleared my mind when, in a then unpublished review, he suggested that it deserved a wider-reaching recognition from an audience somewhat larger than that of the narrow world of climbing.

It is those who have not found an easy fit either with themselves or their surroundings who are always the more likely to move matters on and, characteristically, Menlove Edwards produced a few fragments. 'End of a Climb' and 'False Gods' contain much that could have been developed, but he decided to channel his creative energies elsewhere. There was one group, however, that promised much. From the very beginning, the female climber has had to deal with a variety of problems. One young woman, to cover her visits to the hills, was driven to invent fictional but parentally acceptable holidays, supported by bogus picture postcards. So, confounded by dress codes and patronised at every turn, women climbers had the perfect left-field viewpoint and in due course it produced a rich vein of writing. Dorothy Pilley, Mabel Barker and Gwen Moffat led the way, while Elizabeth Coxhead opened the door to creative climbing fiction.

Given the quality and success of their forebears, it is a surprise and a pity that the literary output from women has apparently not increased at the same exponential rate as that of their male counterparts. In Neate's *Mountaineering Literature* (H167), her revised bibliography of published books, less than five percent had been written by women, and the bibliography that follows this essay shows no significant change. There could be three possible reasons for this:

(a) That Virginia Woolf's objectionable Charles Tansley is more or less right when he says 'Women can't write. Women can't paint.'

(b) The British publishing industry practises the same level of discrimination as the average football fan.

(c) Women have little interest in producing material which merely plods the mainstream path of heroic or mock-heroic endeavour.

The last point will most repay further thought. At one stage in the last century there was a rejection of the concept that endeavour on the hill demonstrated the Graeco–Christian idealism of Man at its most noble, existing in natural harmony with God and Nature, and with this went the belief that an important function of mountain literature was to illustrate this abstract idea in concrete form. Phrases like 'the lift of its sombre precipice above the ruffled lake' quietly slipped out of fashion and in their place grew a more acerbic tone inspired by Swift, polished by the likes of

C E Montague and finally chipped into sharp edges by the class struggles of the Thirties. There weren't many climbing Dorothy Parkers around to stand the female corner and those there were probably had more important targets than men who justified their Boys' Own antics through mockery of self and others.

Nevertheless, there is evidence that if the measure is quality rather than quantity, matters would be cast in a different light. Women form a relatively small part of any sporting congregation—there are not many women writers on football or cricket, for example—and there was the limiting presumption that only those who had achieved particular success in their field had the right to air their experiences in public. But that minority more than held its own when it came to relative ability. Neate's first edition in 1978 employed a star system to indicate particular interest and worth. Ten percent of these were awarded to books written by women, despite their modest individual output. Even this percentage of stars was skewed because men, having their feet under the publishers' table, had the opportunity to be more prolific. The odds were heavily stacked. Perhaps the time had come for a break up the blind side.

At the Millennium, a co-operative of women got together to 'provide a focus for creativity and the publication of [an] annual anthology' and tap into the 'special energy that comes from working with other women'. These words appear in the introduction to the sixth edition of *Women Mountains Words* (H35). This is an eclectic collection, including poetry, prose fiction (serious and otherwise), memoir and literary review. It is difficult to pin down the exact nature of the 'energy' but the opening poem 'The River Esk', where the enthusiasm of a burgeoning river is constrained by the historical obstacles that litter its path, gives a clue. It is even more difficult to work out the chicken and egg element in any chain of causation but it may be more than coincidence that at least two of the contributors to Anthology 6, Judith Brown and Jan Levi, have had the excellence of their work acknowledged by such judges as those of the Boardman Tasker prize and the Climb/International Festival of Mountaineering Literature Writing Competition.

As an aside, I found the review of Nan Shepherd's *The Living Mountain* curiously interesting. The book, written in the late Forties but not published for thirty years, is, with its personal and fond memories of the Cairngorm and its lengthy publishing gestation, reminiscent not only of Wainwright's *A Pennine Journey* (H232) but, more particularly, Fred Whyte's *A Cairngorm Chronicle* (H245) written at around the same time on the same subject. It too delayed its birth and did not appear in print until 2007, and then only through the efforts of his daughter and the enthusiasm of a female publisher. Perhaps that is what is meant in Judith Brown's introduction to *WMW6* when she talks about their efforts hitting 'a chord with men who also aspire to produce the kind of outdoor writing that doesn't fit within [...] the mainstream' and the possible consequent establishment 'of a brother group'.

A final thought on fiction. Coxhead and Harrison have cleared the path. Isn't it about time someone produced a novel that catches the essence of the British mountains as it exists in the brave new world of the 21st century?

Bibliography and Lists

In the pages that follow are the bibliography and lists mentioned in the explanation at the start of this book. Although the official scope of this survey is the twenty-five years between 1983 and 2008, one or two titles have crept in which we feel belong to the chosen cohort but which did not surface until the early months of 2009.

As with all lists, there will be disagreement over books omitted through either accident or design, or books included that do not meet the specifications set. No matter, debate passes the idle hour.

CH/GW

Notes and Abbreviations

The following bibliography specifies the first edition published in the UK but does not include the subsequent print history of each book. With the proliferation of hardback and paperback reprints, this would have been an endless task. Although we have endeavoured to use objective criteria for inclusion (see 'An Explanation', page 1) the final list deviates a couple of times and reflects the occasional personal whim. If you believe something merits inclusion, then we would be delighted to consider it for any subsequent edition. Please contact the publishers through their website (www.millracebooks.co.uk).

General reference sources
o   Booksellers' websites
o   Publishers' websites
o   Numerous new and second-hand bookshops
o   Book dealer catalogues
o   The Boardman Tasker Charitable Trust website
o   Kendal Library Mountaineering Collection

Abbreviations used in this bibliography
abb.   abbreviations
ack.   acknowledgements
ad.   advertisement
b&w   black & white
bio.   biography
chr.   chronology
cm   height of book to the nearest 0.5cm (width indicated in brackets when bigger than height)

col.	coloured
con.	contents
cre.	credits
ded.	dedication
d/j	dust jacket: a removable cover
endp.	endpaper (the very first and last page)
ed.	editor
for.	foreword
frpc.	frontispiece (an illustration/photograph opposite the title page)
glo.	glossary
ills.	photographic illustrations within the text (b&w unless stated). Many modern books have numerous full-page photographic images. These are defined as illustrations (and not plates) when these pages are numbered.
inc.	including
ind.	index
int.	introduction
ISBN	International Standard Book Number. This is a unique number allocated to a particular edition of a book. This was originally a 10-fig. number but since 2007 has been increased to a 13-fig. number. During the transition phase of 2006 both ISBN numbers have been given.
nos.	impression numbers, usually on the publisher page on the reverse side of the title page; a true first edition (i.e. first edition, first impression) has the full sequence of numbers that typically look like the following: 1 3 5 7 9 10 8 6 4 2 or 10 9 8 7 6 5 4 3 2 1 The following would suggest a 3rd impression: 3 5 7 9 10 8 6 4 or 10 9 8 7 6 5 4 3
num.	numerous
p.	numbered pages
pbk.	paperback

plate a glossy page (i.e. generally a different quality paper to the body of text) with one or more photo images. Plate pages are not included in the page numbering and therefore it is not always obvious if they have been removed.

pre. preface

pro. prologue

pub. publisher

quo. quotation

sbk. softback covers with front and rear flaps

Book pagination

Many collectors are rightly keen to know that all the pages that should be in a book are still there. Unfortunately there is no standard method of numbering pages. In the main bibliography the following rules have been adopted:

o It is assumed that all books have a front and rear free endpaper (the first and last blank pages), half-title page (with just the title) and title page (with title, author and publisher). These, and their reverse sides, are rarely numbered. All other pages will be indicated in the listings.

o Pages before or after the main body of text without numbers are indicated within the following brackets [ ]. Example: [3-inc. con. & int.] v-xiii +5-*237*p. [3]. Three pages without numbers (including contents and introduction) follow the reverse side (verso) of the title page; then, starting with v and finishing with xiii, there are numbered preliminary pages using roman numerals; then numbered pages starting with 5 and finishing with 237 (although the last page of the main text is not numbered—indicated with italics); then 3 blank pages before the rear free endpaper. Complex, but not unusual.

1 ALLAN, DAVID &
WHITESIDE, JUDY
*So You Want to Join Mountain
Rescue? Mountain Rescue
Explained*
Kirkby Stephen: Hayloft
Publishing, 2006 (pbk. only).
5-200p., num. cartoons,
18.5cm; (x21.5cm);
ISBN-10: 1904524478 &
ISBN-13: 9781904524472
A book of cartoons by Allan
who is the medical officer and
chairman of Mountain Rescue
(England and Wales).

2 ALLAN, ELIZABETH
*Burn on the Hill: The Story of
the First 'Compleat Munroist'*
Beauly: Bidean Books, 1995.
[4-con., ills. list & ack.] 184p.
[2-Appendix], no d/j issued,
21.5cm; no ISBN stated.
Details the wanderings between 1914 and 1927 of A R G
Burn, the first to complete
every Munro and Top in 1923.
(See also *The First Munroist* by
Drummond and Mitchell.)

3 ALLEN, R F (ed.)
*The Climbers' Club Guidebook
Centenary Journal*
The Climbers' Club, 2009.
3-304p., num. b&w and col.
ills., topo diagrams, 24cm;
ISBN 9780901601865
Celebrating a century of CC
guidebooks that began with the
guide to Lliwedd by Thomson
and Andrews in 1909. A facsimile reprint of this guide is
reproduced in full, followed
by many original articles from
over 20 contributing authors.
Allen has written many walking guides to the mountains,
particularly the Lake District.

4 ALVAREZ, AL
*Feeding the Rat: Profile of
a Climber*
London: Bloomsbury, 1988.
[8-inc. author bio., ded., con.
& ills. list] 13-152p. [6],
8 b&w plates, 22cm;
ISBN 0747501785
Biography of rebellious British
climber Julian 'Mo' Anthoine
(1939–89). 'Feeding the rat'
is an expression he used to
describe what drove him to
court discomfort. He was
drawn to 'deep play' activities,
where what you might lose
seemed out of proportion to

what you might gain. Anthoine set up Llanberis-based Snowdon Mouldings in 1968 and died as a result of a cancerous brain tumour. Alvarez (1929–) was a regular climbing partner of Anthoine and has written other books on subjects such as gambling and suicide.

5 ANDREW, JAMIE
Life and Limb: A True Story of Tragedy and Survival Against the Odds
London: Portrait, 2003. [1-ded.] vi-xiv [2] +3-306p., 8 col. plates, 24cm; ISBN 0749950072
British climbers' epic ascent of the north face of Les Droites in the French Alps in 1999. Jamie Fisher died and Andrew (1969–) subsequently lost all his limbs to frostbite. Some of the later chapters concerning his rehabilitation describe his efforts to return to rock climbing and mountaineering in the UK.

6 ANGELL, SHIRLEY
Pinnacle Club: A History of Women Climbing
The Pinnacle Club, 1988.

[5-inc. ill., ded. & pub. info.] viii-xiv +249p. [9 inc. subscribers and index], ills., pictorial laminated boards, no d/j issued, 25cm; ISBN 0951396706
The Club, formed in 1921 specifically for women's rock climbing, was founded by Eleanor Winthrop Young (daughter of Cecil Slingsby and wife of Geoffrey WY), Emily 'Pat' Kelly and sisters Paddy and Biddy Wells. Angell (1930–) was President of the Club from 1978–81.

7 ASKWITH, RICHARD
Feet in the Clouds: A Tale of Fell-running and Obsession
London: Aurum Press, 2004. frpc. map [4-ded., warning & con.] 339p. [5], 8 plates, nos., 22.5cm; ISBN 1854109898
Journalist Askwith's obsession with completing the Lake District's Bob Graham Round (42 mountains within 24 hours) is interwoven with encounters with legendary British fell runners such as Joss Naylor, Billy Bland, Kenny Stuart and Ian Holmes.

8 ATKINSON, TREVOR
*The MOMMS Mountaineering
Challenge*
Challenge Publications, 2002
(pbk. only). [3-con., ills. list
& photo list] 67p., col. ills.,
diagrams & drawings, 21cm;
ISBN 1903568021
A series of challenges mainly in
the UK by the 'Mountaineers
of Mettle & Mountain Safety
Society' based in North Wales.
They include the Yorkshire
Three Peaks, Welsh Three Thou-
sanders, any 300ft rock climb
and Jack's Rake on Pavey Ark.

9 BAILEY, ADRIAN
*Lakeland Rock: Classic Climbs
with Chris Bonington*
London: Weidenfeld &
Nicolson, 1985. frpc.,
[1-con.] 6-144p., ills.
(mainly col.), 22cm; ISBN
0297786377
Based on the TV series featur-
ing five milestone climbs in
the Lake District, with Don
Whillans, Bill Peascod, Pete
Livesey, Jill Lawrence, Gill
Price, Pete Whillance and
Dave Armstrong all having
starring roles. Both Peascod

and Whillans died of heart
attacks shortly after the book
was published. Bailey is a journalist and photographer.

10 BAND, GEORGE
*Summit: 150 Years of the
Alpine Club*
London: Collins, 2006.
[1-con] 6-256p. num. col. &
b&w ills., endp. ills., 28cm;
ISBN-10: 0007203640 &
ISBN-13: 9780007203642
Large-format history of the
world's first national alpine
club, established in 1857.
It is also the story of British
mountaineering, as many of
the leading participants were
members of the Alpine Club.
Band (1929–) made the first
ascent of Kanchenjunga in
1955 with Joe Brown, was
former President of the Alpine
Club and the BMC, and was
recently awarded the OBE.

11 BARRIE, PATRICIA
Songs of Silence
Dinas Powys: Honno, 1999
(pbk. only). [4-inc. ded.,
pronunciation & poem]
216p. [2-inc. pub. info.];

ISBN 1870206398
Novel set in the Welsh mountains. Short-listed for the Boardman Tasker Prize, although there are no climbing or mountaineering scenes.

12 BARRY, JOHN
The Great Climbing Adventure
Sparkford: Oxford Illustrated Press, 1985. [2-con. & ack.] 251p., 8 col. plates, 22cm; ISBN 0946609071
Barry's (1944–) mountain adventures around the world, with two chapters on British rock and ice. Former Royal Marine and Director of Plas y Brenin National Mountain Centre from 1978–85.

13 BARTLETT, PHIL
The Undiscovered Country: The Reason We Climb
Glasgow: The Ernest Press, 1993. frpc., [4-inc. con. & pre.] 183p., ills., 24cm; ISBN 0948153245 (also limited edition of 100 numbered & signed copies)
A mix of philosophy, history and autobiography from British climber Bartlett

(1955–), with pen-portraits of Doug Scott, Joe Tasker, Peter Boardman, Chris Bonington, Eric Shipton, Bill Tilman, Sir Francis Younghusband and Leslie Stephen.

14 BASSINDALE, JON, SALE, RICHARD, JONES, ANNETTE & BASSINDALE, KEVIN
Holding the Heights: a Rock Climbing Diary
London: Constable, 1987. frpc., 5-191p., ills., 26.5cm; ISBN 0094675309
Sale and K Bassindale follow young enthusiastic climbers Jones and J Bassindale (son of Kevin) through a year of climbing.

15 BAXTER, COLIN & CRUMLEY, JIM
Glencoe: Monarch of Glens
Lanark: Colin Baxter Photography, 1990. 4-96p., pictorial laminated boards matching d/j, num. ills. (mainly col.), 30.5cm; ISBN 0948661151
A portrait of Glencoe reflecting on its history, dramatic

landscape and unrestricted access to the mountains, corries and glens. Over 14,000 acres of Glencoe are now owned by the National Trust for Scotland, largely as a result of the fund-raising appeals of the SMC in the 1930s.

16 BEATTY, JOHN (ed.)
This Mountain Life:
The First Hundred Years
of The Rucksack Club
Bamford: Northern Light, 2003. 116p., ISBN 0954621107
Manchester-based club founded in 1902. Photographic history published to commemorate the Club centenary, edited by a nature, travel and adventure photographer.

17 BELLAMY, REX
Walking the Tops: Mountain Treks in Britain
Newton Abbot: David & Charles, 1984. [2-inc. con.] 7-208p., 16 b&w plates, 22cm; ISBN 0715384198
A personal account of walking on Dartmoor, the Brecon Beacons, Rhinog Fawr, the Peak District and other places, with recollections of people, places, events and history.

18 BELLAMY, REX
The Four Peaks: One Man's Journey to the Summits of Ireland, Scotland, Wales and England
London: MacDonald, 1992. [4-inc. con. & map] 227p. [4], 16 plates, 24cm; ISBN 0356200248
At the age of 62, Bellamy (a sports writer for *The Times*) set off to climb the highest points of Great Britain.

19 BENSON, PETER, CUDAHY, MIKE & GRANT, IAN (eds.)
From Kinder Scout to Kathmandu: a Rucksack Club Anthology 1907–1986
Cheshire: Rucksack Club, 1987. 5-240p., ills., map, drawings, 22cm; no ISBN stated.
An anthology of climbing, walking and exploration articles from the Club's journals, including 'Gritstone Rocks 1921' by Morley Wood and

'A History of the Moss Ghyll Grooves' by H M Kelly.

20 BIBBY, ANDREW
The Backbone of England: Landscape and Life on the Pennine Watershed
London: Frances Lincoln, 2008. [2-con.] 7-208p., num. col. ills., maps, nos., 26cm; ISBN 9780711228252
Journalist Bibby's walk along the English geographical watershed between Kinder Scout and Hadrian's Wall, exploring its wildlife, ecology, geology and culture.

21 BIRKETT, BILL
Lakeland's Greatest Pioneers: 100 Years of Rock Climbing
London: Robert Hale, 1983. [3-con., ded. & ills. list] 8-192p., 12 plates, 5 drawings, 22cm; ISBN 0709005377
Tracing the development of rock climbing in the Lake District through the biographies of eleven British climbers (W P Haskett-Smith, O G Jones, Frederick Botterill, Siegfried Herford, Harry Kelly, A T Hargreaves, Jim Birkett, Bill Peascod, Alan Austin, Arthur Dolphin and Pete Livesey). Birkett, son of Jim and uncle of Dave, was an accomplished climber before concentrating on writing and photography.

22 BIRKETT, BILL
Scafell: Portrait of a Mountain
London: Frances Lincoln, 2007. 160p., 31cm; ISBN 9780711227248
A fully illustrated tribute to England's highest range.

23 BIRKETT, BILL & PEASCOD, BILL
Women Climbing: 200 Years of Achievement
London: A & C Black, 1989 (pbk. only). frpc., 5-192p., ills., 23.5cm; ISBN 0713657197
The story of women in climbing and mountaineering, from the first female ascent of Mont Blanc in 1808 to the achievements of the modern rock superstars. British women featured include Lucy Walker, Nea Morin, Gwen Moffat and Jill Lawrence.

24 BIRTLES, GEOFF (ed.)
Alan Rouse: A Mountaineer's Life
London: Unwin Hyman, 1987. [2-con.] vii-*xi* +12-224p., ills., 8 col. plates, 24cm; ISBN 0044400756
Biographical portraits from mountaineers who knew Rouse (such as Chris Bonington, Rab Carrington, Brian Hall, Paul Nunn and Doug Scott) and compiled by Birtles (1947–), the founder/editor of *Crags* and *High* magazines. Rouse (1951–86) died in a storm on K2 after reaching the summit.

25 BONINGTON, CHRIS
Mountaineer: Thirty Years of Climbing on the World's Greatest Peaks
London: Diadem, 1989. frpc., [1-con.] 6-192 p., num. col. ills., 32cm; ISBN 090637197X
A photographic autobiography of Britain's best-known mountaineer. Bonington (1934–) made notable first ascents of the Central Pillar of Frêney in the Alps (1961), The Old Man of Hoy (1966), and the first British ascent of the Eiger North Wall (1961). He led successful British expeditions on Annapurna South Face (1970) and Everest SW Face (1975). He finally reached the summit of Everest himself in 1985. The first chapter covers his experiences on British rock and ice.

26 BOTT, GEORGE
Call Out: Keswick Mountain Rescue Team– The First Fifty Years
Keswick: KMRT, 1997 (pbk. only). [4-inc. for. & pre.] 44p., ills. (col. & b&w), 20cm; ISBN 0953109801
The KMRT was formed in 1946 after a difficult rescue of Wilfred Noyce on Great Gable.

27 BOWKER, TOM
Mountain Lakeland
London: Robert Hale, 1984. 224p. ills., map, 23cm; ISBN 0709017537
Celebrating the attractions of the Cumbrian region.

28 BRAHAM, TREVOR
When the Alps Cast Their Spell: Mountaineers of the Alpine Golden Age

Glasgow: The In Pinn, 2004. [2-con. & ack.] 314p., 12 plates (col. & b&w), endp. maps, 24cm; ISBN 1903238749
Biographical portraits of Alfred Wills, John Tyndall, Leslie Stephen, A W Moore, Edward Whymper and A F Mummery, pioneering British mountaineers during the Alpine Golden Age (1855–65).

29 BROOKER, W D (ed.)
A Century of Scottish Mountaineering
Scottish Mountaineering Trust, 1988. iii-xii +372p., 72 plates, drawings, ills. endp., pictorial laminated boards, no d/j issued, 24cm; ISBN 0907521215 (also a special edition of 400 numbered copies)
Anthology from the Scottish Mountaineering Club Journal, edited by Bill Brooker (1934–), a pioneering Scottish climber.

30 BROWN, DAVE & MITCHELL, IAN
Mountain Days and Bothy Nights
Ayrshire: Luath Press, 1987 (pbk. only). [2-con. & ded.] 182p. [2-publisher info.], drawings, 20cm; ISBN 0946487154
Nostalgic and anecdotal stories of walking and climbing in the Scottish hills during the 1950s and 60s.

31 BROWN, DAVE & MITCHELL, IAN
A View from the Ridge
Glasgow: The Ernest Press, 1991 (pbk.) [2-con. & ack.] 185p., 5 sketch maps, 15 drawings, 19.5cm; ISBN 0948153113 (also signed and numbered limited edition of 100 hardback copies)
A follow-up to *Mountain Days and Bothy Nights*, exploring the nature of Scottish hill-walking experiences.

32 BROWN, HAMISH M
Climbing the Corbetts
Scotland's 2,500ft Summits
London: Gollancz, 1988. [6-inc. con., abbr. & ills. list] *11-*381p. [3], 8 col. plates, maps, 23.5cm; ISBN 0575043784
Brown MBE (1934–) was

formerly head of centre at Braehead School in Fife and is now a well-known mountaineer, writer, photographer and lecturer. This book is more than just a guidebook; it relates his personal experiences on these 221 summits.

33 BROWN, HAMISH
The Last Hundred:
Munros, Beards and a Dog
Edinburgh: Mainstream Publishing, 1994. [2-con.] 7-191p., num. ills. & plates (mainly col.), 25cm; ISBN 1851586075
A collection of essays about the Scottish mountains. Many have been previously published in magazines, journals and newspapers. Brown has completed several rounds of the Munros, summer, winter and solo.

34 BROWN, HAMISH & BERRY, MARTYN (eds.)
Speak to the Hills:
An Anthology of Twentieth Century British and Irish Mountain Poetry
Aberdeen University Press,
1985. frpc., vii-xxvii [5-inc. quo. & ill.] 3-530p., ills., 23.5cm; ISBN 0080304060 (also special limited subscribers' edition, numbered and signed by the authors)
A monumental collection of over 600 poems by more than 300 writers, both 'professional' poets and poets who are basically walkers and climbers.

35 BROWN, JUDITH (ed.)
Women Mountains Words:
Anthology Issues 1–6
Privately published each year from 2001–06. All have a similar format: ring-bound pbk., 21cm; no ISBN stated.
WMW is a forum for women who want to write about mountains and climbing. The anthologies are a collection of short stories, novel extracts, articles, plays and poems.

36 BROWN, JUDITH
Happy Climbing Tells No Tales:
and other mountain stories
short and tall
Cockermouth: Open Mountain, 2007 (pbk. only). [4-inc. ded. & con.] 114p.,

21cm; ISBN 9780955498008
'... death and terror get the sales.' Twelve short stories from a leading member of the Women Mountains Words group.

37 BURGESS, ALAN & BURGESS, ADRIAN
The Burgess Book of Lies
Seattle: Cloudcap, US, 1994. [6-ded., ack. & con.] 13-463p., 16 col. plates, ills., 23.5cm; ISBN 0938567381 (simultaneously published in Canada by Rocky Mountain Books)
Autobiography of Yorkshire-born twins (1948–). Mainly about high altitude mountaineering in the Himalaya but with a few early references to climbing in the UK.

38 BUTTERFIELD, IRVINE
The Magic of the Munros
Newton Abbot: David & Charles, 1999. frpc., [1-con.] 6-192p., num. col. ills., 24.5cm (x37cm); ISBN 0715308505
A profusely illustrated book portraying the attraction and mystery of the Munros by Butterfield, a Munroist and founder member of the John Muir Trust.

39 BUTTERFIELD, IRVINE
The Call of the Corbetts
Newton Abbot: David & Charles, 2001. frpc., 5-192p., num. col. ills., 25cm (x30cm); ISBN 0715311522
Similar format to *The Magic of the Munros*. A Corbett is a Scottish mountain between 2,500ft and 3,000ft, with 500ft of re-ascent on all sides. Named after Englishman John Rooke Corbett, who became the fourth Munroist in 1930.

40 CALDWELL, CRAIG
Climb Every Mountain: 498 Scottish mountains in one self-propelled journey
London: MacDonald, 1990. v-xvii [2-inc. map] 375p. [7], num. maps, 8 b&w plates; ISBN 0356188094
An account of the first traverse of the Munros and Corbetts in 1985–86. Caldwell (1959–) completed the journey on foot

and bicycle, with only necessary ferry crossings to reach various Scottish islands.

41 CAMPBELL, ROBIN N (ed.)
The Munroist's Companion: An Anthology
Scottish Mountaineering Trust, 1999. ii-viii +328 p., ills., maps, drawings, endp. tables, pictorial laminated boards, no d/j issued, 24cm; ISBN 0907521509
A selection of articles describing the history, theory, philosophy and present practice of Munro climbing.

42 CAMPBELL, STUART B (ed.)
Things Not Seen: An Anthology of Contemporary Scottish Mountain Poetry
Scotland: Aberdeenshire Council, 1999 (pbk. only). ii-ix [3-inc. title] 84p., 21cm; ISBN 1901275078 (ISBN on title page verso is incorrect)
A collection of poems by climbers set against the backdrop of the Scottish hills. The

title is adapted from a chapter heading in W H Murray's *Mountaineering in Scotland*.

43 CARD, FRANK
Whensoever: 50 Years of the RAF Mountain Rescue Service 1943–1993
Glasgow: The Ernest Press, 1993. [8-inc. con., for., int., quo., ack., & ills.] 338p. [3-drawings], ills., maps, endp. ills., 24cm; ISBN 0948153237
History of a volunteer service that turns out in all weathers and under all conditions, hence the slogan on their crest and the title of the book.

44 (CASTLE, THE)
The Castle Mountaineering Club: the First Twenty-One Years
Sheffield: Sheaf Publishing, 1988 (pbk. only). 158p., col. ills., drawings, ISBN 1850480079
Sheffield-based club founded in 1967.

45 CAVE, ANDY
Learning To Breathe
London: Hutchinson, 2005.
[14-inc. ded., con., ills. list,
int. & quo.] 276p. [10], nos.,
16 plates (14 col.), 24cm;
ISBN 009180034X
A memoir focusing on Cave's
(1967–) experiences as a miner
during the 1984–5 miners'
strike and the 1997 ascent of
the North Face of Changabang
in the Himalaya. In 1986 he
quit his job as a miner and
gained a PhD in socio-linguis-
tics. He is now an international
mountain and ski guide and
one of Britain's top alpinists.

46 CAWTHORNE, MIKE
*Hell of a Journey: On Foot
Through the Scottish
Highlands in Winter*
Edinburgh: Mercat Press,
2000 (pbk. only). [8-inc.
con., ills. list, map list, ack.,
pro. & map] 164 p., 16 plates
(12 col.), ills. & maps, 23cm;
ISBN 1841830054
A 143-day walk in the winter
of 1997–98 from Sandwood
Bay to Glencoe, ascending all
135 mountains over 1,000m.

47 CAWTHORNE, MIKE
*Wilderness Dreams: The Call of
Scotland's Last Wild Places*
Neil Wilson Publishing, 2007
(pbk. only). 176p., 23cm;
ISBN 9781903238905
Eight essays about the author's
travels in the Scottish wilder-
ness and mountains over the
last 20 years.

48 CHRYSANTHOU,
MARC & STAINFORTH,
GORDON (eds.)
*The Owl & the Cragrat: Climbs
and Rhymes—an Anthology of
Climbing Poetry*
Hebden Bridge: Stonegold
Publishing, 2004 (pbk. only).
[1-con.] 6-160p., cartoons,
21cm; ISBN 0954710703
One hundred and twenty-nine
climbing poems adapted from
classics such as Kipling's 'If'
and Wordsworth's 'Daffodils'.

49 CLARK, HILARY
Two Boots and a Polybag
Privately published, Wolverhampton: Clark & Howard
Books, 1984 (pbk. only).
212p., ills., drawings & maps,
20.5cm; ISBN 0950955507

Mountaineering and long distance walking reminiscences mainly in the UK, including the Skye Ridge, the Welsh Three Thousanders and the Pennine Way. Clark (1922–2005) was Chief Housing Officer for Wolverhampton and a lifelong Quaker.

50 COCKER, MICHAEL (ed.)

Wasdale Climbing Book: A History of Early Climbing in the Lake District based on contemporary accounts from the Wastwater Hotel, 1863–1919
Glasgow: The Ernest Press, 2006. ISBN 0948153806 (also 100 copies of a deluxe subscriber's numbered and signed edition)
Celebrating the Fell and Rock Centenary. Many of the most significant handwritten entries have been reproduced in facsimile, including Collie's first winter ascent of Steep Ghyll and Herford and Sansom's ascent of Central Buttress.

51 COFFEY, MARIA

Fragile Edge
London: Chatto & Windus, 1989. [6-inc. ded., ack., pro. & quo.] 5-183p. [2], 8 b&w plates, 23.5cm; ISBN 0701134070
Coffey (1952–) had a love affair with Joe Tasker from 1979 until his death on Everest with Peter Boardman in 1982. The first part gives an account of their relationship within the vibrant British climbing scene of the early 1980s. The second part describes her journey with Hilary Boardman to Tibet and Everest Base Camp, retracing the final steps of Tasker and Boardman.

52 COHEN, ROSEMARY

Above the Horizon
London: Allison & Busby, 1997 (pbk. only). [2-sketch maps] 250p., 19.5cm; ISBN 0749003766
Mountaineering adventure in the Himalaya, with early chapters in Scotland, North Wales and the Lake District. Cohen, a medical doctor, has climbed in Europe and America.

53 COLLISTER, ROB
Over the Hills & Far Away
Glasgow: The Ernest Press, 1996 (pbk. only). iv-viii +9-190p., 12 plates, maps, endp. ill., 21cm; ISBN 0948153407
A collection of essays spread over 30 years of mountaineering life. Only some of these concern the UK but include night climbing on King's College Chapel, Cambridge, fell running and solo climbing in North Wales, and a winter ascent of Point Five Gully on Ben Nevis. Collister is an International Mountain Guide and has been guiding since 1976.

54 CONNOR, JEFF
Creagh Dhu Climber: The Life & Times of John Cunningham
Glasgow: The Ernest Press, 1999. frpc., [1-con.] 4-252p. [2], 32 plates (16 col.), pictorial laminated boards, no d/j issued, 24cm; ISBN 0948153547
Cunningham (1927–80) was one of the leading post-war Scottish climbers who helped revolutionise ice climbing by combining front-pointing techniques with short axes that had angled blades. Whilst leading a group of outdoor education students on a sea-level traverse at Gogarth, North Wales, he was swept off the cliff by a wave and subsequently drowned. Connor (1949–) is a full-time sports writer and author.

55 CONNOR, JEFF
Dougal Haston:
The Philosophy of Risk
Edinburgh: Canongate, 2002. [6-inc. quo., con. & ack.] 211p. [3], 16 plates, illustrated endps., nos., 24cm; ISBN 184195215X
Haston (1940–77) was a controversial and enigmatic Scottish climber who still retains cult status. He made the first ascent of the Eiger Direct in 1966 and he and Doug Scott were the first Britons to reach the summit of Everest in 1975. He became Director of the International Mountaineering School in Leysin, Switzerland and died nearby, having been avalanched whilst skiing.

56 COOPER, MARTIN (ed.)
No Nobler County:
A Celebration of Climbing
in Northumberland
The Northumbrian Mountaineering Club, 1995 (pbk. only).
106p., b&w and col. ills.,
ISBN 0050468622
First-hand accounts of nail-
booted ascents in the 1940s to
descriptions of bouldering in
the 1990s.

57 COUPE, EDWIN,
LAGOE, JOHN &
NETTLETON, JOHN
Fifty Years Running: A History
of the Mountain Trial
The Lake District Mountain
Trial Association, 2002 (pbk.
only). 68p., 8 col. plates, ills.,
cartoons, 21cm; no ISBN
stated.
An annual test of navigation
and endurance dominated
by legendary fell runners Joss
Naylor and Billy Bland who
won the event ten and nine
times respectively. Sue Parkin
has monopolised the women's
event with nine wins. Coupe,
Lagoe and Nettleton are serv-
ing officers of the LDMTA.

58 CRAIG, DAVID
Native Stones: A Book About
Climbing
London: Secker & Warburg,
1987. [6-inc. ded., ack. & ills.
list] 213p., 8 plates, 22cm;
ISBN 0436113503
Climbing in the UK by author
and poet Craig (1932–) who
taught creative writing at
Lancaster University. The book
features Bill Peascod, a regular
climbing partner until just
before his death in 1985.

59 CRAIG, DAVID
Landmarks: An Exploration
of Great Rocks
London: Jonathan Cape,
1995. [8-inc. ded., con., ills.
list, & quo.] 13-335p., ills.,
16 plates, nos., 24cm;
ISBN 022403510X
Worldwide travels by Craig,
exploring the impact of great
cliffs and outcrops on the people who have encountered them.
Includes a section on the British
Isles.

60 CRAM, A G (ed.)
100 Years of Rock Climbing
in the Lake District

The Fell and Rock Climbing Club of the English Lake District, 1986. frpc. (x2), [4-con., notes & ills.] 3-225p. [7 ads.], num. ills., drawings, 21.5cm; ISBN 0850280230 (special issue of *The Fell and Rock Journal* Vol XXIV, No. 70, limited to 1000 copies) Celebrating the centenary of W P Haskett Smith's first ascent of Napes Needle, which marked the start of the sport of rock climbing in the Lake District. As well as a full history, there are several articles (new and reprinted) about climbing in the UK, with contributions by, among others, W Heaton Cooper, Bill Birkett, A Harry Griffin, Tom Price and G S Sansom. Many of the photographs are by the pioneering Abraham brothers. Cram was a leading climber in the Lakes during the mid 1960s.

61 CROCKET, KEN
Ben Nevis: Britain's Highest Mountain
SMC Trust, 1986. frpc., [12-inc. con., ills. list, ack., for. & int.] 320p. [2], ills., maps, diagrams, endp. diagrams, pictorial laminated boards, no d/j issued, 24cm; ISBN 0907521169
The definitive history of Ben Nevis by a leading Scottish ice climber during the mid 1970s.

62 CROUCHER, NORMAN
Legless But Smiling: An Autobiography
Cornwall: St. Ives Printing & Publishing, 2000. vi +368p., 20 plates, pictorial laminated boards, no d/j issued; ISBN 0948385340
In 1995 Croucher (1941–) became the first double amputee to summit an 8,000m peak—Cho Oyu.

63 CRUICKSHANK, JIMMY
High Endeavours: The Life and Legend of Robin Smith
Edinburgh: Canongate, 2005. [7-inc. con., poem & int.] 2-374p., 16 plates (b&w and col.), 24cm; ISBN 1841956589
An outstanding Scottish climber, probably best known

for his ascent with Dougal Haston of The Bat on Carn Dearg Buttress, Ben Nevis. Smith (1938–62) made the first British ascent of the Walker Spur but died with Wilfred Noyce in the Pamirs. Cruickshank was an early climbing partner of Smith's.

64 CRUMLEY, JIM
A High & Lonely Place:
The Sanctuary & Plight of the
Cairngorms
London: Jonathan Cape, 1991. [6-inc. ded., con. & ills. list] 11-157p. [3], 24cm; ISBN 0224026828
Exploring the conflict between maintaining the wilderness environment and leisure developments, deer estates, and current forestry practice. Crumley (1947–) was a journalist for 25 years before he began writing books in 1988.

65 CRUMLEY, JIM
Among Mountains
Edinburgh: Mainstream Publishing, 1993. [4-ded., ack., con. & col. ills.] 9-159p., col. ills., 25.5cm;

ISBN 1851585443
Conservation of the landscape and wildlife in his native Scottish mountains.

66 CRUMLEY, JIM
Gulfs of Blue Air: A Highland
Journey
Edinburgh: Mainstream Publishing, 1997. [6-inc. ded., con. & ack.] 11-192p., 16 col. plates, 24cm; ISBN 1851588892
A journey through the Highlands of Scotland, from Sheriffmuir, near Stirling, to Suilven in the far north west, describing Highland history, people, landscape and wildlife.

67 CUNNINGHAM, FRANK
James David Forbes: Pioneer
Scottish Glaciologist
Edinburgh: Scottish Academic Press, 1990. [2-inc. ded.] vii-xi +329p. [2], diagrams, maps, ills., 25cm; ISBN 0707303206
Academic biography by a university professor focusing on Forbes' (1809–68) contributions to glaciology. He was

also a pioneering and influential alpine mountaineer, even though he maintained that the only justifiable reason for climbing mountains was for scientific purposes.

68 CUNNINGHAM, PAT
In Kinder's Mist
Derby: Pecsaeton Publishing, 2007 (pbk. only). 2-130p., 21cm; ISBN 9780955632501
A ghost story set on the Kinder Scout plateau of the Peak District by an ex-RAF pilot.

69 CURRAN, JIM
Suspended Sentences: From the Life of a Climbing Cameraman
London: Hodder & Stoughton, 1991. [12-inc. ded., con., ills., ills. list, maps, chr. & note] 19-191p., ills., 8 col. plates, 24cm; ISBN 0340518170
Autobiographical book from climber, film-maker, author and artist Curran (1943–). His reconstructions of Menlove Edwards' A Great Effort and Smith and Haston's The Bat were noted 1970s films.

70 CURRAN, JIM
High Achiever: The Life & Climbs of Chris Bonington
London: Constable, 1999. [12-inc. ded., con., ills. list, ack., for. & drawing] 264p., 18 b&w plates, 28 drawings, 24cm; ISBN 0094792801
Curran has accompanied Bonington on three expeditions (Kongur in China, Nanga Parbat and St Kilda) with various filming adventures.

71 CURRAN, JIM
The Middle-Aged Mountaineer: Cycling & Climbing the Length of Britain
London: Constable, 2001. [16-inc. ded., con., ills. list, ack., 6 maps & drawing] 203p., 8 col. plates, 15 drawings, maps, 24cm; ISBN 1841192368
A 1,600-mile cycle journey from Muckle Flugga lighthouse on Shetland to Land's End, via a winding route taking in climbs and climbing friends such as Chris Bonington, Terry Gifford, Geoff Birtles and Catherine Destivelle.

72 DAVIS, HUNTER
Wainwright: The Biography
London: Michael Joseph,
1995. [2-inc. con.] vii-xi
+356p., 16 b&w plates,
sketches, ISBN 0718139097
Alfred Wainwright (1907–91)
will be remembered for his
hand-drawn and handwritten
Pictorial Guides to the Lake
District. His authorised biographer Hunter Davis (1936–),
journalist and radio presenter,
had full access to Wainwright's
private letters and unpublished
material.

73 DAVIS, HUNTER
*The Best of A. Wainwright:
A Personal Selection*
London: Frances Lincoln,
2004. [4-con., ills. list,
drawing] 1-376p., num. ills.
drawn by AW, nos., 17.5cm;
ISBN 0711224633
A selection of eighteen fells
with introductions by Davis.

74 DEAN, STEVE
*Hands of a Climber: A Life of
Colin Kirkus.*
Glasgow: The Ernest Press,
1993. frpc., [4-con., poem,

for. & ack.] 278p., num. ills.,
endp. map & ills., diagrams,
22cm; ISBN 0948153210
(also signed limited edition
of 125 copies)
Kirkus (1910–42) was a highly
influential climber during the
1930s. He was particularly
renowned for a series of new
routes on Clogwyn du'r Arddu
some 20 years before Joe Brown
arrived on the scene. He was
killed in active service for the
RAF. Planning officer Dean
(1950–) has repeated most of
Kirkus's notable climbs.

75 DEARDEN, PAUL
Classic Rock Climbs
London: Blandford, 1994.
[2-inc. con] vii-xii +131p.,
16 col. plates, 24cm; ISBN
0713724366
A celebration of extreme
climbs in England and Wales,
from well-known classics to
personal favourites in less popular areas.

76 DEMPSTER, ANDREW
The Munro Phenomenon
Edinburgh: Mainstream
Publishing, 1995. 192p.

ISBN 1851586989
A history of Munro-bag-ging, from Sir Hugh Munro onwards.

77 DRASDO, HAROLD
The Ordinary Route
Glasgow: The Ernest Press, 1997 (pbk.) [4-inc. ded. & con.] 258p., chapter head vignettes, 21.5cm; ISBN 0948153466 (also signed limited edition hardback of 125 copies)
Autobiography based on fifty years of climbing at home and abroad. Drasdo (1932–) was formerly Head of an outdoor pursuits centre in North Wales and a guidebook writer for Lliwedd and the Eastern Crags of the Lakes.

78 DRUMMOND, EDWIN
A Dream of White Horses: Recollections of a Life on the Rocks
London: Diadem, 1987. 4-224p., 8 plates, 23.5cm; ISBN 0906371961
Autobiographical collection of essays and poems. Drummond (1947–) made the first ascent of Gogarth's Dream of White Horses on Anglesey with Dave Pearce in 1968. He climbed many other new routes in the UK, Norway and Yosemite, and made protest climbs on Nelson's Column and the Statue of Liberty.

79 DRUMMOND, PETER & MITCHELL, IAN
The First Munroist:
The Reverend A. E. Robertson:
His Life, Munros & Photographs
Glasgow: The Ernest Press, 1993. frpc., [1-con.] vi-ix +134p., maps, num. ills., 21.5cm (x22cm); ISBN 0948153199
Complements Allan's *Burn on the Hill*. Robertson completed the Munros between 1889 and 1908, and he coined the word 'bagging' in his diaries. Both the authors have also com-pleted the Munros.

80 DUTTON, G J F
The Ridiculous Mountains:
Tales of the Doctor and his Friends in the Scottish Highlands

London: Diadem, 1984. frpc. drawing, iv-vi +7-158p. [2], 22.5cm; ISBN 0906371619 Humorous short stories describing the bizarre adventures in the Scottish Highlands of the Doctor, the Narrator and the Apprentice. Dutton (1924–) formerly edited the SMC Journal.

81 DUTTON, G J F
Nothing So Simple as Climbing
London: Diadem, 1993. [4-inc. con. & pre.] 9-160p., drawings; ISBN 0906371120 The second collection of tales of the Doctor and his hapless companions.

82 EARL, DAVID W
All in a Day's Work: R.A.F. Mountain Rescue in Snowdonia 1944–46
Llanrwst: Gwasg Garreg Gwalch, 1999 (pbk. only). [1] 6-112p., ills., 21cm; ISBN 0863815545

83 ELSE, RICHARD & HALL, BRIAN
The Face: Six Great Climbing Adventures

London: BBC Books, 1998. [2-con. & col. ills.] 7-208p., num. col. ills., diagrams, 25.5cm; ISBN 0563383194 Book to accompany the BBC series. Although only one of the programmes was devoted to a climb in the UK (the Great Arch on Pabbay, Outer Hebrides), other programmes featured British climbers such as Joe Simpson, Andy Parkin, Airlie Anderson and Tony Howard. Else is Britain's most experienced producer-director of outdoor programmes and Hall was co-director of the Kendal Mountain Film and Book Festival.

84 ENTWISTLE, M D
Millican Dalton: A Search for Romance & Freedom
Blackburn: Mountainmere Research, 2004 (pbk. only). [2-con. & ill.] 106p., ills., 21cm; ISBN 0954721306 A biographical tribute to the life and times of 'the Caveman of Borrowdale', also known as the 'Professor of Adventure'. Dalton (1867–1947) was a pioneer rock climber and

mountain guide who lived a Spartan life under canvas, in caves and a woodland hut.

85 FAWCETT, GILL
The Alternative Guide to British Rock Climbing
London: Unwin Hyman, 1988 (pbk. only). [2-con. & ded.] v-vii +232p., cartoons, maps, 19.5cm; ISBN 0044401140
Humorous observations and information about climbing areas, nearby camping, pubs and cafes, and personalities in the 1980s. Gill Fawcett (Kent) was the first English woman to lead E6 and was editor of *On The Edge* magazine.

86 FISHER, HERVEY
From a Tramp's Wallet: A Life of Douglas William Freshfield, D.C.L., M.A. 1845–1934
Banham: The Erskine Press, 2001. frpc., *v*-xi +307p., ills., 24cm; ISBN 1852970693
Freshfield was a distinguished explorer, mountaineer and President of both the RGS and the Alpine Club. Fisher (1927–) is his great grandson.

87 FORBES, GRAHAM
Rock and Roll Mountains
Edinburgh: Mainstream Publishing, 2005 (pbk. only). [4-thanks & con.] 9-223p., 23.5cm; ISBN 9781840189698
Climbing memoirs from an ex-guitarist of the Incredible String Band in the drug-crazed 1960s and 70s, who later discovered the mountains and corporate life. Several chapters concern Scottish adventures.

88 FOWLER, MICK
Vertical Pleasure: The Secret Life of a Taxman
London: Hodder & Stoughton, 1995. [6-inc. ded., con., ack., ills. list] 11-224p., 16 col. plates, maps, nos., 24cm; ISBN 0340623217
Autobiography of *The Observer Magazine*'s 'Mountaineers' Mountaineer', and winner with Paul Ramsden in 2002 of the Piolet d'Or. Fowler (1956–) has successfully juggled his professional and family life with a string of successful climbing forays at home and abroad. The chalk cliffs of southern

England, sea stacks all round the British Isles, and northern Scotland ice are included.

89 GIFFORD, TERRY
The Stone Spiral
Clapham: Giant Steps, 1987 (pbk. only). [2-inc. con.] 7-42p., 21cm; ISBN 0948727020
Most of the poems concern the natural world but a few have a climbing theme.

90 GIFFORD, TERRY & THOMAS, ROSIE (eds.)
Orogenic Zones:
the First Five Years of the
International Festival of
Mountaineering Literature
Wakefield: Bretton Hall, 1994 (pbk. only). [2-inc. ack.] iv +246 +v-xxvii p., 21cm; ISBN 0952469308
Diverse collection of articles and poems by Dave Cook, Janet Adam Smith, Geoff Dutton, Alison Fell, Dennis Gray and Anne Sauvy, etc. Originally based at the Bretton Hall College of the University of Leeds, the annual International Festival of Mountaineering Literature is now incorporated into the Kendal Mountain Festival.

91 GIFFORD, TERRY
The Rope
Bradford: Redbeck Press, 1996 (card covers). [4-inc. ded., ack. & con] 9-52p. [4-inc. publisher info.], 21.5cm; ISBN 0945980276
Thirty-two climbing poems with an emphasis on UK locations.

92 GIFFORD, TERRY (ed.)
The Climbers' Club Centenary Journal
The Climbers' Club, 1997. 3-303p., 72 b&w plates, 24cm; ISBN 0901601675
An anthology of essays from 113 volumes of journals, first produced in 1898. Contributors include O G Jones, George Mallory, Menlove Edwards, Wilfred Noyce, Peter Harding and Jim Perrin. The CC now has eight huts, with three in Snowdonia, and has been involved in the production of rock climbing guidebooks for 100 years.

93 GIFFORD, TERRY
The Joy of Climbing: Terry Gifford's Classic Climbs
Caithness: Whittles Publishing, 2004 (pbk. only). 3-174p., ills., 20 col. plates, 28cm; ISBN 1904445063
A series of articles following Gifford and friends on easier grade climbs, primarily in Britain. Gifford (1946–) is former Director of the annual International Festival of Mountaineering Literature.

94 GILBERT, RICHARD
Lonely Hills & Wilderness Trails
Newton Abbot: David & Charles, 2000. [6-inc. quo., pub. info. & con.] 11-319p., 32 col. plates, 21.5cm; ISBN 0715309226
Thirty-nine articles (many first published in *High* magazine) about his mountain experiences around the world and in Scotland. Gilbert led the first ever British school expedition to the Himalayas in 1977 and collaborated with Ken Wilson on the *Big Walks*, *Classic Walks* and *Wild Walks* series.

95 GILLMAN, PETER
In Balance: Twenty Years of Mountaineering Journalism
London: Hodder & Stoughton, 1989. [8-inc. ded., con., ills. list, note] 13-252p. [4], 8 plates, 22.5cm; ISBN 0340502940
A compilation of articles that first appeared in the *Sunday Times*. Subjects range from the BBC's outside broadcast of climbing on the Old Man of Hoy in 1967 to the early indoor climbing walls, and include climbing personalities such as Crew, Brown, Patey, Bonington, Haston, Boysen and Burke.

96 GILLMAN, PETER & GILLMAN, LENI
The Wildest Dream: Mallory, His Life and Conflicting Passions
London: Headline, 2000. [7-inc. ded., con., family tree & ack.] xii-xiv +306p., 24 plates, map, nos., 24cm; ISBN 074727150X
Biography of George Herbert Leigh Mallory (1886–1924). His body was not found until 1999.

97 GOODWIN, STEPHEN (ed.)
The Alpine Journal 2007: The Journal of the Alpine Club—a record of mountain adventure and scientific observation
The Alpine Club & The Ernest Press, 2007. frpc., vii-xvi [2-inc. col. ill.] 3-434p. [10-inc. 7 ads.], num. col. & b&w ills., maps, 22.5cm; ISBN 9780948153884
Vol 112 and the 150th anniversary edition (1857–2007). Many articles covering recent climbs, area updates, anniversary issues, history and arts, plus book reviews and obituaries. Contributors include Ian Parnell, Simon Yates, Robert Macfarlane, Ken Wilson, Terry Gifford. Features the artwork of Andy Parkin. Former journalist Goodwin has edited the AJ since 2003.

98 GRAY, DENNIS
Mountain Lover
Marlborough: Crowood Press, 1990. x +206p., ills., 24cm; ISBN 1852232722
Second autobiography, following *Rope Boy* (1970), by Gray (1935–) who was the BMC's first ever National Officer and then the General Secretary from 1974–89.

99 GRAY, DENNIS
Tight Rope: The Fun of Climbing
Glasgow: The Ernest Press, 1993 (pbk.) frpc., [2-inc. con.] 183p., ills., 22cm; ISBN 0948153253 (also signed limited edition hardback of 125 copies)
Collection of climbing stories from the 1950s and 60s. Gray shared ropes with many of the foremost climbers of the day, including Arthur Dolphin, Tom Patey, Don Whillans and Joe Brown.

100 GRAY, DENNIS
Slack: The Fun of Climbing (Volume 2)
Dewsbury: Dennis Gray, 1998 (pbk. only). 183p. [3], ills., 21.5cm; ISBN 1871890292
Follow-up to *Tight Rope,* with more anecdotes concerning many of the leading British climbing personalities, mainly in the 1970s and 80s.

101 GRAY, DENNIS
Poems: 'From the Edge'
Privately published and not
dated. Card covers, 40p.
(unpaginated), 21cm; no
ISBN stated.
Forty-six climbing poems by a
widely travelled climber, some
previously published in various climbing club journals.

102 GRAY, DENNIS
Todhra
Leeds: The Flux Gallery Press,
2005 (pbk. only). [2-inc.
con.] 5-179p., 21cm; ISBN
0955015812
Novel about a climber's struggle to come to terms with his
homosexuality in a prejudiced
environment. UK climbing
locations include Mile End
Climbing Wall, North Wales
slate quarries and winter on
Ben Nevis.

103 GRAY, MURIEL
*The First Fifty: Munro-Bagging
Without a Beard*
Edinburgh: Mainstream
Publishing, 1991. 192p.,
col. plates, ills., maps, ISBN
185158353X
Humorous account of Munro
conquests by TV presenter and
columnist (1958–).

104 GREEN, DUDLEY
Mallory of Everest
Burnley: Faust Publishing,
1990 (pbk. only). frpc.,
[4-con.& pre.] 9-141p.
[2-index], ills., 21cm; ISBN
0948558032
This biography came about following Green's broadcast on
Radio 2 in 1986, an appreciation of Mallory on the centenary of his birth.

105 GREGORY, DAVE
A Necklace of Slings
Glasgow: The Ernest Press,
1995. [8-inc. ack., con.,
for., ded. & drawing] 181p.,
drawings, endp. drawings,
21.5cm; ISBN 0948153377
A collection of short stories,
both fact and fiction, mainly
about climbs and mountains in
the UK. Sheffield-born Gregory
(1935–), a retired teacher,
has been associated with the
production of rock-climbing
guidebooks to the Peak District
since the early 1950s.

106 GREIG, ANDREW
The Return of John Macnab
London: Headline Review, 1996. [4-inc. ded. & ack.] 279p.; ISBN 0747217041
A novel about poaching and land access issues; a modern-day re-enactment of Buchan's *John Macnab*. Greig (1951–) is a Scottish author and poet who has also written two Himalayan mountaineering books.

107 GRESHAM, NEIL
Face Dancing: The Rachel Farmer Trust
Twickenham: Sam & Neil, 1993 (pbk. only). 80p., ills. (mainly col.), 21cm (x21cm); ISBN 0952264307
Mainly a photographic tribute to Rachel Farmer who was the first British woman to climb 8a (Raindogs at Malham). She died in 1993, aged 22, after falling from a walkway at Buoux in France.

108 GRESHAM, NEIL & EMMETT, TIM
Preposterous Tales
Twickenham: Sam & Neil, 2005 (sbk. only). Unpaginated, num. col. ills., 29cm; ISBN 1904207375
International climbing escapades between 1999 and 2003 from two of Britain's elite climbers. The first three chapters focus on climbing in the UK, featuring Gresham's repeat of Dawes' seminal Indian Face E9 6C, gritstone extremes in the Peak District, sea-cliff climbing in Pembrokeshire and deep water soloing at Swanage. Gresham is now both a climbing coach and a training columnist for *Climber*. Emmett has progressed to BASE jumping and wing-suit piloting.

109 GRIFFIN, A H
A Lakeland Mountain Diary: From 40 Years in the Guardian's Country Diary
Marlborough: Crowood Press, 1990. ISBN 1852235659
Griffin MBE (1911–2004) wrote his 'Country Diary' column in *The Guardian* for 52 years. It was the longest-running regular feature in British media history.

110 GRIFFIN, A HARRY
The Coniston Tigers: Seventy Years of Mountain Adventure
Wilmslow: Sigma Leisure, 1999. [15-inc. ded., for., bio., pre., ack., con., map & drawing] 2-206p. [2-ads.], 24 plates, maps, drawings; 23cm; ISBN 1850587132
Autobiography focusing on the Coniston Tigers, a group of climbing friends who formed a club in 1931, its base a converted garage near the shore of Coniston Water.

111 GRIFFIN, A HARRY
(ed. Wainwright, M)
A Lifetime of Mountains: The Best of A. Harry Griffin's Country Diary
London: Aurum Press, 2005. frpc., [4-quo. & con.] ix-x +198p., 19.5cm; ISBN 1845131126
One hundred and fifty selected articles.

112 GRIFFIN, A HARRY
(ed. Hardy, Peter)
The High Places: Leaves From a Lakeland Notebook
London: Frances Lincoln, 2008. frpc., [2-con.] 7-224p., num. ills. drawn by A. Wainwright, nos., 20.5cm; ISBN 9780711228290
For nearly 30 years Griffin wrote a weekly feature for the *Lancashire Evening Post*. This selection of articles describes climbing and mountain days and personalities in the Lakeland fells.

113 HANKINSON, ALAN
A Century on the Crags: the Story of Rock Climbing in the Lake District
London: J M Dent & Sons, 1988. [2-inc. ded.] vii-xiv +225p., 32 plates, 24cm; ISBN 0460047558
From the early 1880s and pioneers such as O G Jones, W P Haskett Smith and the Abraham brothers, to the ascent of Incantations E6 6b on Tophet Wall by Pete Whillance and Dave Armstrong in 1984. This book followed Hankinson's (1926–2007) Channel 4 documentary *Century on the Crags*.

114 HANKINSON, ALAN
*Geoffrey Winthrop Young:
poet, mountaineer, educator*
London: Hodder &
Stoughton, 1995. [8-inc. ded.,
quo., con., ack. & note] 365p.
[7], 8 plates, nos., 24cm;
ISBN 034057609X
Young (1876–1958), an outstanding alpinist, lost a leg
during WWI and was instru-
mental in helping to set up
the first climbing guidebooks,
Gordonstoun School, Outward
Bound and the BMC.

115 HARRISON, M JOHN
Climbers
London: Gollancz, 1989.
[8-inc. con., ded., & quo.]
13-221p. [3], 23.5cm; ISBN
057503632X
Novel about a group of climbers set in the troubled times
of unemployment during
the 1980s. This is Harrison's
(1945–) sixth novel. He also
co-authored the instructional
book *Fawcett on Rock* (1987).

116 HAWKRIDGE, JOHN
Up Hill All the Way
London: Michael Joseph,

1991. [6-inc. ded., note, con.
& ills. list] *246*p., 16 plates
(8 col.), ills., 25cm; ISBN
0718134699
Autobiography of a hill walker
born in 1948 with cerebral
palsy. He won 'Man of the
Year' for sporting achievement
in 1989.

117 HEWITT, DAVE
*Walking the Watershed: The
Border to Cape Wrath along
Scotland's Great Divide*
Glasgow: TACit Press, 1994
(pbk. only). 240p., 20cm;
ISBN 0952268019
An 80-day walk of 850 miles
and 330,000 feet of ascent.
Hewitt (1961–) is editor of
The Angry Corrie, a hill walk-
ing fanzine.

118 HEWITT, DAVE (ed.)
*A Bit of Grit on Haystacks:
A Celebration of Wainwright*
Disley: Millrace, 2004. [4-inc.
ack. & con.] 168p., 17.5cm;
ISBN 1902173171
A collection of ten essays by
outdoor writers, paying trib-
ute to Lakeland legend, Alfred
Wainwright.

119 HITCHEN, PAUL (ed.)
"999 Mountain Rescue, please":
GMRT's 50th Anniversary
1957–2007
Glossop: Bay Tree Books,
2007 (pbk. only). [4-inc.
quo., ded. & con.] *162*p. [4],
ills., ISBN 0955137716
Light-hearted look at rescues
by the Glossop Mountain
Rescue Team.

120 HOLLETT, DAVID
The Pioneer Ramblers:
1850–1940
North Wales Area of the
Ramblers Association,
2002 (pbk. only). ISBN
1901184544
A history of the ramblers'
movement.

121 HUBANK, ROGER
Hazard's Way
Glasgow: The Ernest Press,
2001 (pbk.) 5-248p. [6],
22cm; ISBN 0948153636
(also numbered & signed
limited edition hardback
of 100 copies; ISBN
0948153652)
A novel set around 1900
at Wasdale Head, with a
background of the Boer War.
Real-life climbing characters
(Oppenheimer, Collie, Montague and the Abrahams) are
woven into the story. Hubank's
first novel was an Alpine
climbing adventure *North Wall*
(1977).

122 HUBANK, ROGER
Taking Leave
Glasgow: The Ernest Press,
2004 (pbk. only). 7-269p.,
21.5cm; ISBN 094815375X
Novel about an ex-climber
seeking refuge in the Peak
District whilst coming to
terms with the breakdown of
his marriage.

123 HUMBLE, ROY M
The Voice of the Hills: The Story
of Ben Humble, MBE
Bishop Auckland: The
Pentland Press, 1995. frpc.,
[2-inc. quo. & ded.] vii-xiv
+231p. [2-appendix], ills.,
24cm; ISBN 1858212499
Humble (1903–77) was totally
deaf for most of his adult life.
He qualified in dental radiol-
ogy and eventually turned to
writing, having been inspired

by a visit to Skye. A climbing history, *The Cuillin of Skye*, was published in 1952. His main legacy is his influence on safety in the Scottish hills. Roy Humble (1930–) is his nephew.

124 HURST, IAN & BENNETT, ROGER
Mountain Rescue: history and development in the Peak District, 1920s—present day.
Stroud: Tempus Publishing, 2007 (pbk. only). [2-con. & poem] *7-128*p., num. ills., 8 col. plates, 23.5cm; ISBN 9780752440910

Chronicles the development of the rescue service, covering significant rescues, geography of the area, helicopters used, cave rescues, SARDA dogs, and training. Both authors have been members of the Edale MRT and held organisational posts for the Buxton team.

125 JENKINS, DULCIBEL (ed.)
Chronicles of John R. Jenkins 1913–1947: Mountaineer, Miner and Quaker
Privately published by author, 1987 (pbk. only). Signed limited edition of 250 copies. 3-336p., ills., sketches, drawings, 21cm; ISBN 0951313800

Extracts from mountaineering, mining and social articles, edited by his widow. Jenkins died during a descent of Mont Blanc.

126 JONES, DAVID B A
The Power of Climbing
Winster: Vision Poster Co., 1991. frpc., 7-192p., num. ills., drawings, 28.5cm; ISBN 1873665008

Interviews with over forty elite British climbers (who have climbed the eighth grade) from the 1980s, including Dawes, Dunne, Leach, Moffatt, Moon, Nadin, Pollitt and Pretty. Jones (1960–) was assistant cameraman on feature films such as *Batman* and *Memphis Belle*.

127 JONES, GRIFF RHYS
Mountain: Exploring Britain's High Places
London: Michael Joseph/

Penguin Books, 2007. frpc., [1-con.] 6-256p., num. col. ills., 25cm; ISBN 9780718149895 Book to accompany the BBC series following Jones (1953–), the well-known TV star, across Britain's highlands.

128 JONES, TREVOR & MILBURN, GEOFF
Welsh Rock: 100 Years of Climbing in North Wales
Glossop: Pic Publications, 1986. frpc., [6-inc. col. ills., con., int. & quo.] 9-318p., num. ills. (col. and b&w), pictorial laminated boards, no d/j issued, 25cm; ISBN 095111140X (also special edition of 500 copies signed by both authors)
Profusely illustrated history by Jones (1930–96) and Milburn, a prolific guidebook writer.

129 JONES, TREVOR & MILBURN, GEOFF
Cumbrian Rock: 100 Years of Climbing in the Lake District
Glossop: Pic Publications, 1988. frpc., [4-inc. con., ack. & ills.] 7-257p., 32 col. plates, num. ills., endp. maps, pictorial laminated boards, no d/j issued, 25cm; ISBN 0951111426 (also limited edition of 250 copies signed by both authors)
Following a similar format to *Welsh Rock*.

130 KEMP, PETER
Of Big Hills and Wee Men
Edinburgh: Luath Press, 2004 (pbk. only). 220p., 20.5cm; ISBN 1842820524
Autobiography recounting tales of walking in the Scottish mountains with companions from Kemp's days of working in the dying shipbuilding industry of Glasgow.

131 KENNY, ANTHONY (ed.)
Mountains: An Anthology
London: John Murray, 1991. [6-inc. con., ills. list, quo. & ill.] 357p., b&w wood engravings, 24cm; ISBN 0719546397
Mainly Alpine but some extracts by Keats, Ransome, Lunn, Murray, Noyce and Wainwright concern Britain. Sir Anthony

Kenny (1931–) is an eminent philosophy professor.

132 KIRKPATRICK, ANDY
Psychovertical
London: Hutchinson, 2008.
[6-ded., line ill., con., ills. list & ack.] 277p., 16 col. plates, line ills., drawings, nos., 24cm; ISBN 9780091920968
Autobiography of Kirkpatrick (1972–) renowned for his bold Alpine solo ascents and as an entertaining communicator of his climbing experiences.

133 KIRKUS, GUY
Poems of a Climber
Caergybi: The Ernest Press, 1993 (card covers). 125 signed and numbered copies. 8p., no ISBN stated.
Colin Kirkus' younger brother Guy (1913–) had this booklet of three poems published for the 7th International Festival of Mountaineering Literature at Bretton Hall, Yorkshire.

134 LANE, BRONCO
Military Mountaineering: A History of Services Mountaineering 1945–2000
Kirkby Stephen: Hayloft Publishing, 2000.
[3-inc. ack. & con.] 8-296p. [2], num. ills. (col. and b&w), map, 24cm; ISBN 0952328216
Former SAS soldier Lane (1945–) and Brummie Stokes were the second British team to reach the summit of Everest (1976).

135 LANGLEY, BOB
Fellrunner
Sutton: Severn House, 1996. 256p., ISBN 0727848895
Wartime thriller about a Lakeland fell runner.

136 LARKIN, STEVE
Doing the Wainwrights: 214 Fells, Four Seasons and a Caravan
Studley: Know the Score Books, 2007 (pbk. only).
iii-vii +183p., 32 col. plates, 21.5cm; ISBN 9781905449347
Sixty-three year-old Larkin, who has a medical history, attempts to climb within twelve months all the 214 fells over 1,000 feet, as described

by Wainwright in his *Pictorial Guides*.

137 LEVI, JAN
And Nobody Woke Up Dead: The Life & Times of Mabel Barker—Climber & Educational Pioneer
Glasgow: The Ernest Press, 2006. frpc. drawing, [2-con.] 7-264p., endp. letters, 16 b&w plates, 22.5cm; ISBN-10: 0948153830 & ISBN-13: 9780948153839
Barker (1885–1961) was taught to climb by Millican Dalton in the Lake District. She climbed with the best climbers of the day and made the fourth ascent of Scafell's Central Buttress. Levi is a teacher and co-founder of the Women Mountains Words group.

138 MACFARLANE, ROBERT
Mountains of the Mind: A History of a Fascination.
London: Granta Books, 2003. [6-inc. ded., quo. & con.] 306p. [4], ills., nos., 24cm; ISBN 1862075611
Macfarlane's (1976–) cultural history of the Western love affair with mountains and a personal memoir.

139 MACFARLANE, ROBERT
The Wild Places
London: Granta Books, 2007. [8-inc. ded., quo., con. & ill.] 3-340p. [2], ills., endp. maps, nos., 20.5cm; ISBN 978862079410
Journeys in search of the wildness left in Britain and Ireland.

140 MACGREGOR, RALPH
Hills of the North Rejoice!
Thurso: Curlew Cottage Books, 2004 (pbk. only). viii +212pp, ISBN 095387032424
A collection of essays on adventurous escapades in the Highlands of Scotland. Based on material from the column 'Out and About with Ralph' from the *Caithness Courier*. The title comes from a 19th-century hymn by Charles Oakley.

141 MACINNES, HAMISH
Beyond the Ranges: Five Years in the Life of Hamish MacInnes
London: Gollancz, 1984. [10-inc. note, con. & ills. list] 3-202p. [2], 24 plates (8 col.), maps, 23.5cm; ISBN 0575035129
Adventures in the Andes, Alps and Scottish Highlands, including his work as Safety Officer for some BBC Outside Broadcasts and a film starring Sean Connery. MacInnes (1931–), who is a world authority on mountain rescue, manufactured the first all-metal ice axe and invented the Terrordactyl ice tool. He made the first ascent of Zero Gully, Ben Nevis, with Patey and Nicol in 1957.

142 MACINNES, HAMISH
Sweep Search
London: Hodder & Stoughton, 1985. 5-192p., 8 b&w plates, 22cm; ISBN 0340372583
A sequel to *Call-Out* (1973) with another collection of true mountain rescue stories from the west of Scotland. It spans the period from when dogs were first used to the advent of helicopter rescue.

143 MACINNES, HAMISH
The Price of Adventure: More Mountain Rescue Stories from Four Continents
London: Hodder & Stoughton, 1987. [6-inc. ded., con. & ills. list] 11-192p., 8 plates, 22cm; ISBN 0340263237
With two chapters on Scottish rescues and another on his own close encounter on the Bonatti Pillar of the Petit Dru with Whillans and Bonington in 1958.

144 MACINNES, HAMISH
Murder in the Glen: A Tale of Death and Rescue on the Scottish Mountains
Glencoe: Glencoe Productions, 2008 (pbk. only). [2-inc. list of characters] 249p., 21.5cm; ISBN 9780951438015

Novel set in the West High-lands of Scotland during the 1970s.

145 MACLENNAN, HUGH DAN
The Ben Race: The Supreme Test of Athletic Fitness
Fort William: Ben Nevis Race Association, 1994 (pbk. only). xvi +218p., ills., 25cm; ISBN 0952445328
A history of this annual September event attracting up to 600 racers. The up and down record currently stands at 1hr., 25mins., 34secs.

146 MADGE, TIM
The Last Hero: Bill Tilman— a Biography of the Explorer.
London: Hodder & Stoughton, 1995. [16-inc. ded., quo., con., maps & ack.] 21-288p., 8 plates, maps, nos., 24cm; ISBN 0340584416
H W Tilman (1898–1977) made the first ascent of Nanda Devi in 1936 and, with Eric Shipton, was one of the great 20th-century explorers and travel writers.

147 MASLEN-JONES, B
Countdown to Rescue
Glasgow: The Ernest Press, 1993 (pbk.) frpc., [2-con.] 5-221p., ills., maps, endp. maps, 22cm; ISBN 0948153229 (also signed limited hardback edition of 125 copies)
Search and rescue incidents from Maslen-Jones' (1921–) personal experiences of mountain rescue work in Snowdonia.

148 MASLEN-JONES, B
A Perilous Playground: Misadventures in Snowdonia and the Development of the Mountain Rescue Services 1805–1990s
Wrexham: Bridge Books, 1998 (pbk. only). [8-inc. for., ack., abb., map, con. & int.] 11-208p., endp. maps, ills., 21cm; ISBN 1872424651
A follow-up to *Countdown to Rescue*.

149 MAWER, SIMON
The Fall
London: Little Brown, 2003. [2-inc. ack.] 442p., 22.5cm; ISBN 0316725242

Novel set partly in wartime Britain and partly in the anarchic world of British rock climbing in the early 1970s. Mawer (1948–) taught biology before turning to writing. *The Fall* was inspired by a personal 220ft fall on the north-east face of Ben Nevis.

150 MCNEISH, CAMERON (ed.)
The Book of the Climbing Year
Wellingborough: Patrick Stephens, 1988. [4-inc. con. & int.] 9-152p., ills. (col. and b&w), nos. & endp. ills., 25cm; ISBN 1852600438
A collection of articles by twelve well-known climbers celebrating climbing around the world. British rock and ice is well represented by Ken Crocket, Terry Gifford, David Craig, Jim Perrin and Hamish Brown. McNeish is a well-known hill walker and broadcaster, and editor of *TGO* magazine.

151 MCNEISH, CAMERON & ELSE, RICHARD
The Edge: 100 Years of Scottish Mountaineering

London: BBC Books, 1994. 5-128p., 16 col. plates, ills., 25.5cm; ISBN 056337084X
History and profiles of such climbing personalities as Dave Cuthbertson and Rab Anderson.

152 MCNEISH, CAMERON
The Wilderness World of Cameron McNeish: Essays from Beyond the Black Stump
Glasgow: The In Pinn, 2001. 192p., 23.5cm; ISBN 9781903238301
A collection of essays about his worldwide travels to various wild places, including his native Scotland.

153 MILBURN, GEOFF (ed.)
The First Fifty Years of the British Mountaineering Council: A Political History
Manchester: BMC, 1997. frpc., iii-xiv +321p. [3-ads], 70 plates (3 col.), 22.5cm; ISBN 0903908077 (also limited edition numbered and signed by George Band, John Hunt, Joe Brown and Chris Bonington)

A comprehensive history with contributions by many authors and with a selection of articles from the BMC's magazine *Mountaineering*. The BMC was established in 1944 by Geoffrey Winthrop Young and Leo Amery (successive Alpine Club Presidents). Milburn has taken a prominent role in the production of BMC climbing guidebooks and was editor of the *Climbers' Club Journal*.

154 MILBURN, GEOFF
Helyg: Diamond Jubilee 1925–1985
The Climbers' Club, 1985. 256p., ills. (mainly b&w), 22cm; ISBN 0901601381 (also signed & numbered limited edition of 500 copies) Helyg is the Climbers' Club cottage in the Ogwen Valley, North Wales, discovered by Herbert Carr and opened in 1925. A compilation of material from early Bulletins and Journals by authors such as Raymond Greene, Menlove Edwards, Eric Shipton, Wilfred Noyce and Winthrop Young.

155 MILL, CHRISTINE
Norman Collie: A Life in Two Worlds. Mountain Explorer and Scientist 1859–1942
Aberdeen University Press, 1987. [2-inc. ded.] vii-xiv, +197p., ills., 23.5cm; ISBN 0080324568
Collie was one of the great mountaineers around 1900, with many first ascents in the Alps, Arctic Norway, the Canadian Rockies and the Himalaya. Perhaps he will be remembered best for first ascents of Scafell's Moss Ghyll, Tower Ridge on Ben Nevis and The Cioch on Skye. A distinguished scientist, he pioneered the development of the neon light and X-ray photography.

156 MITCHELL, IAN
Second Man on the Rope: More Mountain Days with Davie
Edinburgh: Mercat Press, 1992 (pbk. only). 136p., ills., 21cm; ISBN 1873644019
Anecdotal short stories.

157 MITCHELL, IAN
Mountain Footfalls: A Calendar of the Scottish Hills

Edinburgh: Mercat Press, 1996 (pbk. only). [4-inc. ded. & con.] ix-x +125p., drawings, 21cm; ISBN 1873644531

Stories based in the bothies and mountains of Scotland.

158 MITCHELL, IAN
Scotland's Mountains before the Mountaineers
Edinburgh: Luath Press, 1998 (pbk. only). xii +201p., 8 col. plates, maps, 21cm; ISBN 0946487391

The history of exploration and ascents, cartography, the evolution of the landscape and the social history of the Scottish Highlands.

159 MITCHELL, IAN
The Mountain Weeps: Thirteen Exercises
Stobcross Press, 1997 (pbk. only). [2-ded. & biog.] 123p., 23.5cm; ISBN 0952974207

Thirteen mountain-focused stories set mainly in Scotland.

160 MITCHELL, W R
After You, Mr. Wainwright: In the Fell Country of Lakeland
Giggleswick: Castleberg, 1992 (pbk. only). 144p., ISBN 1871064651

Reminiscences about Wainwright, with accounts of how the author climbed several of AW's favourite Lakeland fells, and describing the peaks, history and past walkers. Bill Mitchell MBE (1928–) is a prolific writer about the natural history and people of the Yorkshire Dales and former editor of the magazines *The Dalesman* and *Cumbria*.

161 MOFFATT, JERRY
(with Niall Grimes)
Revelations
Sheffield: Vertebrate Publishing, 2009. [6-inc. ded., con. & ills. list] 242p. [4], 16 plates (mainly col.), 24cm; ISBN 9781906148119

Autobiography of one of the world's best climbers during the 1980s. Revelations, on Raven Tor in the Peak District, was the world's first 8a+ when Moffatt made the first ascent in 1984.

162 MORAN, MARTIN
The Munros in Winter:
277 Summits in 83 Days
Newton Abbot: David &
Charles, 1986. 240p., 16
col. plates, ills., maps, 24cm;
ISBN 0715388363
In 1984–85 Moran made
the first winter round of
the Munros. He is a British
Mountain Guide with many
first ascents in Scotland and
the Indian Himalaya, and
former record-holder of the
Cuillin Ridge traverse.

163 MURRAY, SHEILA
The Cairngorm Club
1887–1987
Aberdeen: The Cairngorm
Club, 1987 (pbk. only). ISBN
095122090X
Centenary celebrations recording its foundations and development from the Club's first
lady President.

164 MURRAY, W H
Scotland's Mountains
Scottish Mountaineering
Trust, 1987. xi +305p., num.
ills. (col. and b&w), maps,
pictorial laminated boards,
no d/j issued, 24cm; ISBN
0907521150
Geology, natural history and
walkers' and climbers' routes.

165 MURRAY, W H
The Evidence of Things Not
Seen: A Mountaineer's Tale
London: Bâton Wicks, 2002.
frpc., [2-con.] 7-352p., 40
plates (27 col.), ills., maps;
24.5cm; ISBN 1898573247
Autobiography of Scottish
mountaineer (1913–96), posthumously edited and expanded
by his widow, Anne. Murray
revitalised Scottish winter climbing during the inter-war years
and his books *Mountaineering*
in Scotland (1947) and
Undiscovered Scotland (1951)
are generally accepted as classics
of mountain literature concerning the British Isles.

166 NAYLOR, JOSS
Joss Naylor MBE Was Here:
A personal account of the
complete traverse of the
'Wainwright' Lakeland peaks
Braithwaite: KLETS, not
dated. 30p., ills., 17cm; no
ISBN stated.

In 1986 Naylor completed the traverse of all the summits listed in the seven Lakeland guidebooks written by Wainwright: 214 tops in just under seven days, covering about 391 miles with 121,000ft of ascent—an impressive feat for a 50 year-old.

167 NEATE, JILL
Mountaineering Literature: A Bibliography of Material Published in English
Milnthorpe: Cicerone Press, 1986, 2nd edition (pbk. only). i-xiii +14-296p., ills., 21.5cm; ISBN 0902363824
First published as *Mountaineering and its Literature* in 1978 by W R Neate (1934–93), these editions are an essential part of any collector's library.

168 NELSSON, RICHARD (ed.)
The Guardian Book of Mountains
London: Guardian Books, 2007. frpc., [2-inc. con.] vii-viii +264p., ills., 19.5cm; ISBN 9780852650790
A collection of articles on mountaineering and climbing written between 1903 and 2007 for *The Guardian*. Contributors include E A Baker, A H Griffin, Jan Morris, Jim Perrin and Ed Douglas. Nelsson is chief librarian for *The Guardian* and *The Observer*.

169 NOBLE, TIM
Great VS Climbs in the Lake District
Newton Abbot: David & Charles, 1989. frpc., [2-con. & col. ill.] 6-160 p., ills. (col. & b&w), 27cm; ISBN 0715392476
Teacher and climber Noble (1950–) links Lakeland climbs and walks to form a series of strenuous and challenging mountain days that attempt to recapture the romantic spirit of the Victorians.

170 NOLAN, ALAN
Ancient Feet: There's Life in the Old Legs Yet!
Leicester: Matador, 2008 (pbk. only). 272p., 21cm; ISBN 9781906510978
The humorous adventures of five men attempting to follow

Wainwright's Coast to Coast walk across northern England.

171 NUNN, PAUL
At the Sharp End
London: Unwin Hyman, 1988. vi +201p., num. ills., 25.5cm; ISBN 0044401388
A selection of articles written from over thirty years of climbing and mountaineering around the world. Nunn (1943–95) was Chairman of the BMC at the time of his death on Haromosh II in the Karakoram.

172 PEASCOD, BILL
Journey After Dawn: The Autobiography of Climber/ Artist Bill Peascod
Milnthorpe: Cicerone Press, 1985. [10-inc. ded., con., ills. list, for., ack. & pro.] 173p. [5], 16 b&w plates, 24cm; ISBN 0902363689
Peascod (1920–85) was a pioneer Lakeland climber before the Second World War and subsequently became a renowned artist.

173 PERRIN, JIM
Mirrors in the Cliffs
London: Diadem, 1983. frpc., 5-688p., 32 plates (11 col.), 22.5cm; ISBN 0906371953
A follow-up to *The Games Climbers Play* (1978). A collection of over 100 mountaineering essays, extracts and poems edited by Perrin (1947–) with an all-star cast of contributors. The title comes from the Menlove Edwards' essay 'End of a Climb'.

174 PERRIN, JIM
Menlove: The Life of John Menlove Edwards with an appendix of his writings
London: Gollancz, 1985. [10-inc. ded., quo., con., ills. list & for.] 15-347p. [5], 16 plates, 23.5cm; ISBN 0575035714
Influential climber during the inter-war years, with many first ascents in North Wales. Edwards was a psychiatrist and conscientious objector, and in his last years paranoid schizophrenia contributed to his eventual suicide.

175 PERRIN, JIM
On and Off the Rocks:
Selected Essays 1968–1985
London: Gollancz, 1986.
frpc., [3-con. & photo list]
8-192p., num. ills., 24cm;
ISBN 0575038101
Most of the essays are articles
from climbing magazines and
club journals on the theme
of people and mountains in
the UK. Also biographical
portraits of H W Tilman, Pat
Littlejohn, Jill Lawrence, Al
Harris, Chris Bonington and
others.

176 PERRIN, JIM
Yes, To Dance: Essays from
Outside the Stockade
Sparkford: Oxford Illustrated
Press, 1990. [3-con. & ack.]
6-196p. [4], ills., 24.5cm;
ISBN 1855092174
A second collection of essays.
Perrin has a degree in English
and Welsh, a PhD in English
Political Biography and was
a leading climber in the
1970s before turning to full-
time writing. 'Yes, to dance
…' comes from Dylan's 'Mr
Tambourine Man'.

177 PERRIN, JIM
Spirits of Place: Travel,
Encounters and Adventures
in Wales.
Llandysul: Gomer Press,
1997. frpc., [3-ded. & con.]
8-250p. [2], ills., 25cm; ISBN
1859024823
An assortment of articles, from
climbing in Cornwall to Cadair
Idris, and the funeral address
of climber Paul Williams.

178 PERRIN, JIM
Travels with The Flea:
and Other Eccentric Journeys
Glasgow: The In Pinn, 2002
(pbk. only). [4-inc. ded.
& con.] xi-xxi +248p., 24
col. plates, 23.5cm; ISBN
1903238366
In the title essay Perrin follows
in the footsteps of the 19th-
century travel writer George
Borrow through the hills and
wild places of mid-Wales,
accompanied by his dog, Flea.
The rest are a collection of
worldwide travel essays.

179 PERRIN, JIM
The Villain: The Life of Don
Whillans

London: Hutchinson, 2005. [6-inc. ack., con. & ills. list] xi-xiv +354p., 16 plates, nos., 24cm; ISBN 0091794382
Biography of British climber and mountaineer (1933–85) who made a legendary contribution to climbing in the UK, Alps, Himalaya and Patagonia. His inventions, the Whillans Harness and Whillans Box (a rigid expedition tent), were influential equipment designs.

180 PERRIN, JIM
The Climbing Essays
Glasgow: The In Pinn, 2006. [4-inc. ded. & quo., author info. & con.] xiii-xvi +320p., 8 b&w plates and 8 col. plates, 24cm; ISBN-10: 1903238471 & ISBN-13: 9781903238479
Memoirs featuring a collection of Perrin's essays from four decades of climbing.

181 PRETTY, HARRY (ed.)
Oread Mountaineering Club: 50th Anniversary Journal 1949–1999
Derby: Oread Mountaineering Club, 1999. xii +322p., 8 col. plates, ills., sketches, 24.5cm; ISBN 0953573605
Extracts from Newsletters and Journals of the Peak District-based club, supplemented by contemporary essays, edited by Pretty who was a founder member. Oread means mountain nymph.

182 PRICE, TOM
Travail So Gladly Spent
Glasgow: The Ernest Press, 2000. frpc., [2-con.] 7-280p., drawings & ills. endp., 21.5cm; ISBN 0948153563
A collection of articles from Price (1919–), former warden of Outward Bound Eskdale. Although he was widely travelled, many of these articles are concerned with British mountains and outdoor education issues. The title comes from a poem by Sir Thomas Wyatt, 'Forget Not Yet'.

183 PRITCHARD, PAUL
Deep Play: A Climber's Odyssey from Llanberis to the Big Walls
London: Bâton Wicks, 1997. frpc., 5-192p., 16 col. plates, diagrams, drawings, 23.5cm;

ISBN 189857314X
Autobiography from a leading 1980s and 90s climber. Shortly after the book was published Pritchard's (1967–) life was dramatically changed by a serious accident on the Totem Pole in Tasmania.

184 REDHEAD, JOHN
... and one for the crow: (words and images of ascent)
Llanberis: Serious Clowning Publications, 1996. [8-inc. ack., con., photo list, route list, for. & commentary] 154p. [2], ills., col. sketches, 30.5cm; ISBN 0948385286
The art and essays of climber Redhead (1953–) and the photography of Ray Wood, featuring 40 extreme climbs (E3–E8) in North Wales. The Master's Wall/Indian Face controversy on Clogwyn du'r Arddu with Johnny Dawes made climbing headlines in the late 1980s.

185 RICHARDSON, SHEILA
The Forgotten Man of Lakeland
Cumbria: Mill Field Publications, 1997 (pbk.

only). 183p., b&w ills., 21cm; ISBN 0952666545
(also limited signed & numbered edition)
Biography of William T Palmer (1877–1954), an original member of the Fell and Rock Climbing Club and a prolific author on outdoor life, folklore and customs in the Lake District and many other parts of Great Britain.

186 RICHARDSON, SHEILA
The Team: The Story of the Cockermouth Mountain Rescue Team 1953–2003
Cumbria: Mill Field Publications/CMRT, 2002 (pbk. only). 234p., 8 col. plates, ills., 21cm; ISBN 095266657X
A history to celebrate the CMRT's 50th anniversary by a Lakeland author.

187 ROBINSON, JEREMY ROWAN
The Long Day Done
Kirkby Stephen: Hayloft Publishing, 2003 (pbk. only). [2-quo. & map] 5-173p.,

21cm; ISBN 1904524036
Mountain rescue novel based in the Lake District. Robinson was formerly a member of the Langdale/Ambleside MRT and solicitor to the National Park authority.

188 ROBSON, ERIC
After Wainwright: a 190-mile adventure through the mountains of remote Lakeland
Cumbria: Striding Edge, 2003. 205p., 17cm; ISBN 0946812039
Robson's memoir of his days on the hill with Britain's best known fell walker, recalled during a 190-mile adventure in the Lakeland mountains. Broadcaster Robson is the current chairman of Radio 4's *Gardeners' Question Time*.

189 ROSE, DAVID & DOUGLAS, ED
Regions of the Heart: The Triumph and Tragedy of Alison Hargreaves
London: Michael Joseph, 1999. [6-inc. ded., quo. & con.] xi-xii +290p. [2], 8 plates, nos., 24cm;

ISBN 0718144066
When Hargreaves (1962–95) died on K2, she was both maligned and admired for her climbing achievements, driven by commercial pressures and the needs of her family. Three months before her death she made the first unsupported ascent of Everest by a woman without bottled oxygen. Rose and Douglas are both climbers and freelance writers. The title is adapted from a line in a Winthrop Young poem 'Knight Errantry'.

190 SALKELD, AUDREY & SMITH, ROSIE
One Step in the Clouds: an omnibus of mountaineering novels and short stories
London: Diadem, 1990. frpc., iv-vi +7-1056p., nos., 23.5cm; ISBN 0906371929
Thirty-one short stories (including Montague's celebrated 'In Hanging Garden Gully'), one play, two novellas, four novels (Coxhead, *One Green Bottle*; Hubank, *North Wall*; Salter, *Solo Faces*; Harris, *Vortex*) and a comprehensive

bibliography. Salkeld (1936–) is a renowned mountaineering historian, scriptwriter, translator and Boardman Tasker Prize winner. Smith (1954–) has worked for *Mountain*, *On The Edge* and the BMC.

191 SCOTT, DOUG
Himalayan Climber:
A Lifetime's Quest to the
World's Greater Ranges
London: Diadem, 1992. frpc., [1-con] 6-192p., num. col. ills., endp. ills., 32cm; ISBN 0906371937
A photographic autobiography of one of the most prolific Himalayan mountaineers. Most expeditions were without bottled oxygen, alpine-style on huge peaks. Scott (1942–) will be best remembered for the ascent of Everest SW Face in 1975 and his epic descent of The Ogre with two broken legs in 1977. He now champions the causes of the Tibetan and Nepalese native peoples.

192 SCROGGIE, SYDNEY
The Cairngorms Scene and Unseen
Scottish Mountaineering Trust, 1989. 177p., ills., drawings, laminated pictorial boards, no d/j issued; ISBN 0907521258
Autobiographical work of a renowned hill walker, poet and scholar (1919–2006). It describes Scroggie's return to walking and climbing in the hills after being left blinded and one-legged when he stepped on a mine during the Second World War. He featured on TV's *This is Your Life* in 1964.

193 SCULTHORPE, HAROLD
Freedom to Roam
London: Freedom Press 1993 (pbk. only). [2-con. & ills. list] 7-80p., 16 plates, 20.5cm; ISBN 0900384689
Short essays reflecting on the constraints placed on walkers by a host of bureaucratic bodies, including the military, large landowners and water companies. Sculthorpe is a retired lecturer in Biological Sciences.

194 SELLERS, GLADYS &
MAKIN, TONY
*Fifty Years of Caving and
Climbing with the Lancashire
Caving and Climbing Club
1936–1986*
Lancashire CCC, 1986. 104p.

195 SELWOOD, MARY-
JANE (ed.)
*On the Edge of Silence:
A Mountain Anthology*
Helensburgh: Springbank
Press, 1993. 79p., col. &
b&w ills., 22cm; ISBN
095219760X
Poems and excerpts from
Wordsworth, Tennyson, Rus-
kin, Winthrop Young, Larkin
and many others, with colour
reproductions of mountain
landscape paintings by Sarah-
Jane Selwood and half-tone
illustrations by Helmut Fabini.

196 SHARP, BOB &
WHITESIDE, JUDY
Mountain Rescue
Kirkby Stephen: Hayloft
Publishing, 2005 (sbk. only).
[2-con. & col. ill.] 5-263p.,
b&w and col. ills., ISBN
1904524397

History, stories and information on UK mountain rescue.
Sharp is a retired University
Reader and has been actively
involved in Scottish mountain
rescue for over thirty years.
Whiteside, a freelance copy-
writer and illustrator, is a non-
operational member of the
mountain rescue organisation.

197 SIMPSON, JOE
This Game of Ghosts
London: Jonathan Cape,
1993. frpc., [6-inc. con., ills.
list, quo. & ills.] *11-320*p.,
num. ills., nos., 24cm; ISBN
0224035150
Memoirs from *Touching the
Void* author (1960–). From
childhood influences to life
and death experiences in the
Alps and higher ranges, with a
host of other British climbing
personalities.

198 SISSONS, DAVID (ed.)
*The Best of the Sheffield
Clarion Ramblers' Handbooks:
'Ward's Piece'*
Tiverton: Halsgrove, 2002.
3-208p., ills., 24cm; ISBN
1841142220

The SC Rambling Club was formed in 1900 and the miniscule handbooks were written and edited almost single-handedly by Bert Ward (1876–1957) from 1902 until his death. They contained Peak District walking information, local history, folklore, anecdotes, geology and access information. Ward's Piece was an area of land on Lose Hill given by the Ramblers' Association to Ward, who subsequently gave it to the National Trust. Sissons works for Sheffield Libraries, Archives and Information Services.

199 SISSONS, DAVID (ed.)
Right to Roam: A Celebration of the Sheffield Campaign for Access to Moorland
Northend/SCAM, 2005 (pbk. only). 88p., ISBN 0901100609
Newly opened access areas with routes pioneered by the well-publicised mass trespasses of the past.

200 SLESSER, MALCOLM
With Friends in High Places:
An Anatomy of Those Who Take to the Hills
Edinburgh: Mainstream Publishing, 2004. [2-inc. ded.] 7-256p., 8 col. plates, maps, 24cm; ISBN 1840188480
Autobiography from Professor Slesser (1926–2007) who was a scholar in the field of energy studies and had a climbing career spanning 64 years. With John Hunt he co-led the 1962 expedition to the Pamirs during which Smith and Noyce were killed.

201 SMITH, BILL
Stud Marks on the Summit: A History of Amateur Fell Racing 1861–1983
Privately published, SKG Publications, 1985 (pbk. only). [18-inc. con., map list, map, pre., ack. & key to names of athletic clubs] 1-581p., 32 plates, maps, 21.5cm; no ISBN stated.
A comprehensive history, mainly concerned with races and runners from the traditional racing areas of Northern England and Scotland.

202 SMITH, ROGER (ed.)
*The Great Outdoors Book
of the Walking Year*
Wellingborough: Patrick
Stephens, 1988. [2-con. &
ill.] 7-192p., endp. ills., num.
ills., 16 col. plates, nos.,
25.5cm; ISBN 0850599350
Twelve contributors write
about a place of special
meaning, from January in
the Lakeland Fells to July in
the Scottish Highlands and
December in the Yorkshire
Dales. Smith edited *TGO*
magazine for nine years and
organises the annual Scottish
coast to coast *TGO* Challenge.

203 SMITH, ROLY (ed.)
*A Sense of Place: The Best
of British Outdoor Writing*
London: Michael Joseph,
1998. frpc. drawing, v-*xviii*
+*221*p., drawings, 22.5cm;
ISBN 0718142063
A collection of eighteen previously unpublished essays
on the contributors' favourite
places in the British countryside. Includes climbing in
the Avon Gorge by Stephen
Venables, the Ochil Hills

by Rennie McOwan and
Dartmoor by Richard Sale.
Smith is President of the
Outdoor Writers' Guild, a
prolific author of books on
the British countryside and
formerly worked for the Peak
District National Park.

204 SMITH, ROLY (ed.)
*Kinder Scout: Portrait of
a Mountain*
Derbyshire County Council,
2002 (sbk. only). 3-144p.,
num. col. ills., 21cm; ISBN
0903463687
A book originating from an
exhibition of photographs
by Stephen Lewis, including
chapters on natural history,
recreational activities, access
history (and the famous Mass
Trespass in 1932), and modern
management.

205 SMITH, ROLY
*A Camera in the Hills: The Life
and Work of W A Poucher*
London: Frances Lincoln,
2008. [2-con. & for.] 7-192p.,
num. b&w and col. ills.,
26cm; ISBN 9780711223986
Biography of Poucher (1891–

1988), a pioneering landscape photographer and the 'Father' of British perfumery. (He was for thirty years Chief Perfumer at Yardley.)

206 SOMERS, DERMOT
Mountains and Other Ghosts
London: Diadem, 1990. [4-inc. con. & intro.] 9-224p., 23.5cm; ISBN 0906371686
Retrospective collection of short stories, many featuring mountains with a political dimension. Irishman Somers (1947–) made successful ascents of the six great Alpine north faces in 1982 and 1983.

207 SOMERS, DERMOT
At the Rising of the Moon
London: Bâton Wicks, 1994 (pbk. only). [2-inc. con.] 7-208p., 23cm; ISBN 1898573050
Ten short stories with mountain and climbing themes.

208 STAINFORTH, GORDON
Eyes to the Hills: The Mountain Landscape of Britain
London: Constable, 1991.
[8-ded., con., title & col. ills.] 13-207p., num. col. ills., 30cm; ISBN 0094706107
Large-format book of mountain landscape and climbing photography. Stainforth (1949–) is a freelance photographer, writer and Fellow of the RGS.

209 STAINFORTH, GORDON
Lakeland: Landscape of Imagination
London: Constable, 1992.
[1-con.] 6-192p., num. col. ills., map, 30cm; ISBN 0094718008
Photography accompanied by selected literary quotes.

210 STAINFORTH, GORDON
The Cuillin: Great Mountain Ridge of Skye
London: Constable, 1994.
frpc., [1-con.] 6-176p., num. col. ills., 30cm; ISBN 0094715505
Mountain photography of the 'British Alps', with a detailed guide to the main traverse of the Cuillin Ridge.

211 STAINFORTH, GORDON
The Peak: Past and Present
London: Constable, 1998. frpc., [1-con.] 6-224p., num. col. ills., 30cm; ISBN 0094754209
A personal perspective of the UK's first national park, with a large section devoted to the Peak's climbing history. It includes photographs of Joe Brown (aged 66) repeating his own The Right Unconquerable on Stanage Edge and Peter Harding (aged 71) on Valkyrie at the Roaches.

212 STEELE, PETER
Eric Shipton: Everest and Beyond
London: Constable, 1998. [10-inc. ded., quo., con., ills. list, map list & letter] 290p., maps, drawings, 16 plates, 24cm; ISBN 0094783004
Arguably the greatest 20th-century mountain explorer, Shipton (1907–77) is best known for his lightweight Himalayan expeditions with H W Tilman. He made the first traverse of Mount Kenya in 1930, was in the summit party that climbed Kamet during Smythe's expedition in 1931 (the highest summit then attained), was leader of the highly successful Everest Reconnaissance of 1935, and in latter years made six expeditions to the Patagonian ice-cap. British-born Steele (1935–) was the doctor on the controversial 1971 International Everest Expedition and has lived in the Yukon Territory since 1975.

213 STEPHENSON, TOM
(ed. Ann Holt)
Forbidden Land: The Struggle for Access to Mountain and Moorland
Manchester University Press, 1989. 243p., 21.5cm; ISBN 0719028914
Stephenson (1893–1987) was a journalist and long-time secretary of the Ramblers' Association promoting walkers' rights.

214 STOKES, BRUMMIE
Soldiers and Sherpas: A Taste for Adventure
London: Michael Joseph,

1988. [2-con. & ills.] 250p.,
32 plates (24 col.), endp. maps,
24cm; ISBN 0718131193
Autobiography of John Henry
Stokes (1945–), who in 1976
was the third/fourth Briton to
ascend Everest with fellow SAS
climber Bronco Lane.

215 STORER, RALPH
The Joy of Hillwalking
Ayrshire: Luath Press, 1994
(pbk. only). x +139p. [11-inc.
pub. ads], drawings, 21cm;
ISBN 0946487286
Exploring the lure of the hills,
particularly in Scotland. Hill-
walking guidebook writer
Storer (1947–) formerly lec-
tured in computer studies.

216 SUMMERS, JULIE
*Fearless on Everest: The Quest
for Sandy Irvine*
London: Weidenfeld &
Nicolson, 2000. frpc., [2-inc.
ded.] vii-xii +290p. [2], 24
plates, maps, 24cm; ISBN
0297646826
A biography of Mallory's partner on Everest, written by
Irvine's (1902–24) great niece.

217 SYMONDS, HUGH
*Running High: The First
Continuous Traverse of the
303 Mountains of Britain
and Ireland*
Moffat: Lochar Publishing,
1991. ISBN 0948403918
A 2,000-mile run in 97 days
over 277 Scottish Munros,
four English tops, fifteen
Welsh peaks and seven Irish
summits.

218 THOMSON, ALAN
Glencoe: The Changing Moods
Moffat: Lochar Publishing,
1990. 10 full-page ills. before
title page [3-inc. con. & ills.]
16-120p., num. b&w and col.
ills., ISBN 0948403268
Thomson (1939–) is a mem-
ber of the Glencoe Mountain
Rescue Team, and a photo–feature writer. This largely reflects
the content of the book.

219 THOMSON, I D S
*The Black Cloud: Scottish
Mountain Misadventures
1928–1966*
Glasgow: The Ernest Press,
1993 (pbk.) 274p., ills., maps,
22.5cm; ISBN 0948153202

(also signed limited edition hardback of 125 copies)
From a time when searches were made by shepherds and stalkers, to the use of helicopters and trained mountain rescue teams. By writer Ian Thomson (1945–).

220 THOMSON, I D S
May the Fire be Always Lit: A Biography of Jock Nimlin
Glasgow: The Ernest Press, 1995 (pbk.) [2-con. & ills.] 210p., 12 plates, 21cm; ISBN 0948153393 (also signed limited edition hardback of 100 copies)
Nimlin (1909–88) was a pioneering Scottish climber in the 1920s and 30s who founded the Ptarmigan Mountaineering Club. He made many first ascents, particularly at Arrochar and Glencoe.

221 TOWNSEND, CHRIS
The Great Backpacking Adventure
Sparkford: The Oxford Illustrated Press, 1987. [4-con., ack. & int.] 225p., 8 col. plates, 22cm;

ISBN 0946609292
Backpacking memoirs include the Pennine Way, Land's End to John O'Groats and Munro peak-bagging. Townsend is the current President of The Mountaineering Council of Scotland and Equipment Editor of *TGO* magazine.

222 TOWNSEND, CHRIS
The Munros and Tops: A Record-setting Walk in the Scottish Highlands
Edinburgh: Mainstream Publishing, 1997. 224p., 24.5cm; ISBN 1851589864
The first continuous journey of all 277 Munros and 240 Tops in the Scottish Highlands (118 days, 1,700 miles walking and cycling and 575,000ft of ascent).

223 TRAVIS, PETER
The Round
Privately published. Preston: TKI Publications, 1988 (pbk. only). 239p., drawings, endp. author biog. & map, 18cm; no ISBN stated.
A fictional story based in the Lake District, about an ex-

teacher's quest to complete the 24-hour Bob Graham Round. Ex-teacher, fell runner Travis (1933–) also had several poems published in the magazine *The Fell Runner*.

224 TREACHER, KEITH
Siegfried Herford:
An Edwardian Rock-Climber
Glasgow: The Ernest Press, 2000. frpc., [1-con.] 6-168p., ills., drawings, endp. ills., 22cm; ISBN 0948153520
Treacher's (1923–) biography of Herford (1891–1916), who was killed tragically young on active service at Ypres. He was recognised as the finest British rock climber of that era. In 1914, with Sansom, Gibson and Holland, he made the first ascent of the Central Buttress of Scafell. For many years it remained the most difficult rock climb in Britain.

225 TULLIS, JULIE
Clouds From Both Sides
London: Grafton Books, 1986. [10-inc. ded., ack., con., poem, map, chart & diagram] 306p., 20 plates

(16 col.), maps, diagrams, 23.5cm; ISBN 0246127716
Autobiography (1939–86) of the first British woman to climb an 8,000m peak. Tullis partnered Kurt Diemberger on several expeditions and died on K2 during the infamous storm of 1986.

226 TURNBULL, RONALD
The Book of the Bivvy
Milnthorpe: Cicerone, 2001 (pbk. only). frpc., [1-con] 6-139p. [5-inc ads.], ills., maps, 17.5cm; ISBN 185284342X
An instructive, historical and humorous look at the art of bivvying in the mountains of Britain. Turnbull is a writer and photographer.

227 TURNBULL, RONALD
The Riddle of Sphinx Rock:
The life and times of Great Gable
Disley: Millrace, 2005. [6-inc. ack., advice, con. & map] 181p., drawings, ills., 17.5cm; ISBN 1902173198
A cultural history of Great

Gable and its walking, scrambling and climbing routes. The mountain receives about 20,000 ascents each year and, with the FRCC war memorial plaque on the summit, is particularly popular on Remembrance Day.

228 TURNBULL, RONALD
The Life and Times of the Black Pig: A biography of Ben Macdui
Disley: Millrace, 2007. [4-ded., advice & con.] *184*p., drawings, 17.5cm; ISBN 9781902173252
Seventeen ways up Scotland's second highest mountain, plus history, science and fairy stories.

229 UNSWORTH, WALTER
This Climbing Game: an Anthology of Mountain Humour
Viking, 1984. 220p., sketches, 22.5cm; ISBN 0670800570
Nearly fifty extracts that illustrate the humour of climbing, including Claude Benson, John Barry, Tom Patey,

H W Tilman and Mark Twain. Unsworth (1928–) was editor of *Climber and Rambler* and author of many other climbing and walking books.

230 VENABLES, STEPHEN
Higher Than the Eagle Soars: A Path to Everest
London: Hutchinson, 2007. [10-inc. ded., con., ills. list. & ack.,] 370p., 16 col. plates, nos., 24cm; ISBN 9780091795610
Autobiography culminating in his ascent of Everest without bottled oxygen in 1988. Venables (1954–) was President of the AC during its 150th anniversary and is now a full-time writer, broadcaster and public speaker.

231 WAINWRIGHT, ALFRED
Memoirs of a Fellwanderer
Michael Joseph, 1993. 210p., ills., sketches, maps, ISBN 0718140656
The story behind Wainwright's *Pictorial Guides,* illustrated with his distinctive drawings. The material, some of

which appeared previously in *Fellwanderer* (1966) and *Ex-Fellwanderer* (1987), has been combined to produce this memoir.

232 WAINWRIGHT, ALFRED
A Pennine Journey: The Story of a Long Walk in 1938
London: Michael Joseph, 1986. viii +213p., ISBN 0718127307
A solitary walk from Settle to the Roman Wall along the eastern flank of the Pennines, and returning on the west side. This account of a pre-war escape to the hills and a 'blissful interlude of freedom' remained in a drawer for nearly fifty years before being published.

233 WAINWRIGHT, ALFRED
Ex-Fellwanderer: A Thanksgiving
Kendal: Westmorland Gazette, 1987. 160p., ills., ISBN 0902272640
Autobiographical reminiscences published to celebrate his 80th birthday.

234 WAINWRIGHT, ALFRED
Wainwright's Favourite Lakeland Mountains
London: Michael Joseph, 1999. 216p., ISBN 0718133706
Thoughts on twenty Lakeland fells.

235 WAINWRIGHT, MARTIN
The Man Who Loved the Lakes
London: BBC Books, 2007 (pbk. only). 192p., 24cm; ISBN 9781846072949
A tribute to the life of Wainwright and his Lakeland fell experiences, with a selection of walks featured in the BBC series *Wainwright's Walks*. Martin Wainwright is not related to AW.

236 WAINWRIGHT, J A
A Deathful Ridge: a novel of Everest
Oakville: Mosaic Press, Canada, 1997. [6-inc. ded., quo. & ack.] 138p., 21.5cm; ISBN 0889626502
Speculative novel where a distraught Mallory is found alive

on Everest and secretly taken back to Britain to live in silence for another 22 years.

237 WALLER, MICHAEL
A Lakeland Climbing Pioneer: John Wilson Robinson of Whinfell Hall
Bookcase, 2008 (pbk. only). 148p., b&w ills., 21cm; ISBN 9781904147350
Biography of a farmer and businessman (d. 1907), who climbed Pillar Rock over 100 times. The nearby Robinson's Cairn was built as a memorial by his friends.

238 WATSON, JIM
On Foot & Finger: Climbing & Walking Cartoons
Milnthorpe: Cicerone Press, 1986 (pbk. only). 102p. (unpaginated), 11.5cm (x17.5cm); ISBN 0902363816

239 WATSON, JIM
On More Feet & Fingers
Milnthorpe: Cicerone Press, 1987 (pbk. only). 102p. (unpaginated), 11.5cm (x17.5cm); ISBN 0902363964

A second collection of climbing and walking cartoons from Cumbrian-born former engineering draughtsman.

240 WATSON, PETER
Rivington Pike: History and Fell Race
Sunnydale Publishing, 2001 (pbk. only). 192p., 20.5cm; ISBN 0954031709
An annual race, since 1892, up a Lancashire hill. In 2008 it attracted nearly 300 competitors.

241 WEIR, TOM
Weir's World: an Autobiography of Sorts
Edinburgh: Canongate, 1994. 8-248p., 32 plates (16 col.), 24cm; ISBN 0862414806
Tom Weir MBE (1914–2006) was a Scottish climber, author, broadcaster and campaigner for the protection of the environment.

242 WELLS, COLIN
A Brief History of British Mountaineering
The Mountain Heritage Trust, 2001 (pbk. only). v-viii

+120p., ills., 21cm (x29.5cm);
ISBN 090390862X
Mainly concerns British
mountaineers in the higher
ranges but a few chapters are
about Britain.

243 WELLS, COLIN
Who's Who in British Climbing
Buxton: The Climbing
Company, 2008 (pbk. only).
ii-v +575p., b&w ills., 21cm;
ISBN 9780955660108
Nearly 700 short biographies
of mainly British-born climbers and mountaineers. Wells
is Reviews Editor of *Climb*
magazine.

244 WHITE, JOHN
*Rescue! True Stories from
Lake District Mountain Rescue*
London: Constable, 1997.
[4-ded., ack., con. & ills.
list] 9-211p. [5-inc. map],
8 b&w plates, 24cm; ISBN
0094767203
White was a National Park
Ranger and rescue team
member before running a
mountaineering school in the
Lakes.

245 WHYTE, A F
A Cairngorm Chronicle
Disley: Millrace, 2007.
[14-inc. drawing, con., ack.,
for., poem & int.] 157p.,
endp. maps, 17.5cm; ISBN
9781902173238
Written in the 1940s, these are
reflections on mountain days
in the Cairngorms stretching
back nearly 50 years.

246 WILSON, GRAHAM
*Macc and the Art of
Long Distance Walking*
Disley: Millrace, 1998.
[4-inc. ack. & con.] 152p.,
drawings, 17.5cm; ISBN
1902173015
Part I focuses on walking in
the Macclesfield ('Macc') area
and Part II on the Derwent
Watershed, the Welsh Three-
thousanders and the Bob
Graham Round, with diver-
sions into mountaineering
literature. Wilson (1939–) is a
retired teacher of English.

247 WILSON, GRAHAM
Climbing Down
Disley: Millrace, 2002. [4-inc.
ack. & con.] 160p., drawings,

17.5cm; ISBN 1902173120
More humorous and 'rambling digressions' in a similar vein to *Macc & the Art of Long Distance Walking*.

248 WILSON, GRAHAM
Macc and Other Islands
Disley: Millrace, 2004.
[4-inc. ack. & con.] 182p.
[2-inc. author & pub. info.],
drawings & endp. drawings,
17.5cm; ISBN 1902173155
Lyrical and satirical essays, mainly featuring Scottish islands but also climbing on Pillar Rock and a pen-portrait of Millican Dalton.

249 WILSON, GRAHAM
(ed.)
The Central Buttress of Scafell
Disley: Millrace, 2004. [4-inc. ack. & con.] 183p., drawings, 17.5cm; ISBN 1902173163
A collection of early FRCC and YRC essays charting the history of this legendary route, first ascended by Herford, Sansom, Gibson and Holland in 1914 (now given E3 since the loss of the chockstone in 1994).

250 WILSON, GRAHAM
A Measure of Munros
Disley: Millrace, 2005.
[4-inc. ack. & con.] 181p.
[3-inc. author & pub. info.],
drawings & endp. drawings,
17.5cm; ISBN 190217318X
Idiosyncratic look at Munros and the Munro-bagging obsession.

251 WILSON, GRAHAM
A Rope of Writers: A look at mountaineering literature in Britain.
Disley: Millrace, 2006. [4-inc. ack. & con.] 184p., 17.5cm; ISBN-10: 1902173228 & ISBN-13: 9781902173221
A diverse tour of mountaineering literature, club journals and guidebook writing, from O G Jones to Jim Perrin.

252 WILSON, GRAHAM
Tops of the North, Vol I: Three Shire Head to Carlisle
Disley: Millrace, 2008.
[4-inc. ack., con. & map] 176p., drawings, 17.5cm; ISBN 9781902173269
Part I of a high-level walk that travels the moors and fells,

taking in county tops (old and new) of northern England.

253 WILSON, K, ALCOCK, D & BARRY, J (eds.)
Cold Climbs: the Great Snow and Ice Climbs of the British Isles
London: Diadem, 1983. frpc., v-xv +16-280p., num. ills. (mainly b&w) & diagrams, 28cm; ISBN 0906371163
The fifth in the series (starting with *Hard Rock*) covering different aspects of British mountaineering. Sixty-five anecdotal and descriptive essays of mainly Scottish winter climbs, with contributions by Patey, Nunn, Fyffe, Marshall, Boysen, Carrington and many others. Wilson (1941–), photographer and Bâton Wicks publisher, is a well-known personality in the British climbing scene. Alcock (1939–) and Barry (1944–) both formerly worked for Plas y Brenin (the National Centre for Mountain Activities).

254 WILSON, KEN & NEWMAN, BERNARD (eds.)
Extreme Rock: Great British Rock Climbs
London: Diadem, 1987. frpc., iv-xii +13-296p., num. ills. (mainly col.) & diagrams, 28cm; ISBN 0906371368
The sixth in the series, this one celebrating the rock-climbing renaissance of the 1980s, with many climbers such as Fowler, Livesey, Littlejohn, Rouse and Redhead contributing descriptive essays about modern classics from E1 to E7. Newman (1950–) is the current editor of *Climber* magazine.

255 WILSON, KEN (ed.)
Classic Rock: Great British Rock Climbs
London: Granada, Bâton Wicks, 2007. frpc., 4-296p., num. ills. (mainly col.), endp. ills., 31.5cm; ISBN 9781898573708
Technically a second edition but a significant update of an influential book first published in 1978. Showcasing the best traditional climbs in the easier grades, with greater use of colour photography and historical inserts, but using most of the original articles by well-known climbing personalities.

256 WOLLASTON, NICHOLAS
My Father, Sandy
London: Short Books, 2003. [2-inc. quo.] 7-191p., ills., nos., 22.5cm; ISBN 1904095445
Biography of A F R Wollaston (1875–1930) by his son, who was just four when his father, a Cambridge don, was shot and killed at King's College by a disturbed undergraduate. Wollaston, a geographer and naturalist, made expeditions to the Ruwenzori, Dutch New Guinea and Everest.

257 WOOD, RAY
On This Mountain: Essays on Ten Welsh Mountains
Llandysul, Gomer Press, 2008. [7-inc. quo., con., pref. & col. ill.] 2-110p., num. col. ills., 22.5cm (x25cm); ISBN 9781843239161
Celebrating the mountains of Wales, Wood's photographs accompany contributions from Jim Perrin and others. Wood is one of the UK's foremost outdoors photographers.

258 YATES, SIMON
The Flame of Adventure
London: Cape, 2001. [8-inc. ded., con., ills. list, quo. & map] 220p. [6], 8 col. plates, nos., 24cm; ISBN 0224060457
Mountaineering travelogue from Yates (1963–), best known as Simpson's climbing partner in *Touching the Void*. Mainly about mountaineering in the higher ranges but he has climbed with many well-known British climbers and there is a chapter on rope access work in London.

Boardman Tasker Prize
Winners and short-listed books

The Boardman Tasker Charitable Trust was established to promote literature by awarding an annual prize to authors of literary works primarily concerned with mountains. To qualify, the books must be distributed in the UK.

For each year below, the first-named book won the award and the others were on the short-list. Titles without a bibliographical reference number (e.g. H172) do not appear in the main bibliography because they are not primarily concerned with mountain literature about Britain.

1983   (No award made.)

1984   Joint winners: *Living High: A Family Trek in the Himalayas.* Linda Gill, Auckland: Hodder & Stoughton, and *The Shishapangma Expedition.* Doug Scott & Alex Macintyre, London: Granada.

1985   Winner: *Menlove: The Life of John Menlove Edwards with an Appendix of his Writings.* Jim Perrin, London: Gollancz. (H174)
Journey After Dawn: The Autobiography of Climber/Artist Bill Peascod. Bill Peascod, Milnthorpe: Cicerone Press. (H172)
Summit Fever: The Story of an Armchair Climber on the 1984 Mustagh Tower Expedition. Andrew Greig, London: Hutchinson.

1986   Winner: *Painted Mountains: Two Expeditions to Kashmir.* Stephen Venables, London: Hodder & Stoughton.
Kingdoms of Experience: Everest, the Unclimbed Ridge. Andrew Greig, London: Hutchinson.

On and Off the Rocks: Selected Essays 1968–1985. Jim Perrin, London: Gollancz. (H175)

Savage Snows: The Story of Mont Blanc. Walt Unsworth, London: Hodder & Stoughton.

1987   Winner: *In the Footsteps of Scott.* Roger Mear & Robert Swan, London: Jonathan Cape. (Journey to the South Pole)

K2, Savage Mountain, Savage Summer. John Barry, Sparkford: Oxford Illustrated Press.

Native Stones: A Book About Climbing. David Craig, London: Secker and Warburg. (H58)

1988   Winner: *Touching the Void.* Joe Simpson, London: Jonathan Cape. (Peruvian Andes epic)

Feeding the Rat: Profile of a Climber. Al Alvarez, London: Bloomsbury. (H4)

K2, Triumph and Tragedy. Jim Curran, London: Hodder & Stoughton.

Thin Air: Encounters in the Himalayas. Greg Child, Wellingborough: Patrick Stephens.

1989   Winner: *Climbers.* M John Harrison, London: Gollancz. (H115)

Everest, Kangshung Face. Stephen Venables, London: Hodder & Stoughton.

1990   Winner: *Elusive Summits: Four Expeditions in the Karakoram.* Victor Saunders, London: Hodder & Stoughton.

Footloose in the Himalayas. Mike Harding, London: Michael Joseph.

Mountains and Other Ghosts: Short Stories by … Dermot Somers, London: Diadem. (H206)

Vortex. David Harris, London: Diadem; although first published in *One Step in the Clouds* by Salkeld & Smith, London: Diadem, 1990. (North Cascades fiction)

1991   Joint winners: *Mer de Glace.* Alison Fell, London:
Methuen (Alpine fiction) and *A View from the Ridge.*
Dave Brown & Ian Mitchell, Glasgow: The Ernest Press.
(H31)
*Suspended Sentences: From the Life of a Climbing Camera-
man.* Jim Curran, London: Hodder & Stoughton. (H69)
The Endless Knot: K2, Mountain of Dreams and Destiny.
Kurt Diemberger, London: Grafton.

1992   Winner: *In Monte Viso's Horizon: Climbing All the Alpine
4000m Peaks.* Will McLewin, Glasgow: The Ernest Press.
*Flammes de Pierre: Short Stories About Mountains and
Mountaineers.* Anne Sauvy, London: Diadem.
My Vertical World: Climbing the 8000-metre Peaks. Jerzy
Kukuczka, London: Hodder & Stoughton.
*Spirit of the Age: The Biography of America's Most
Distinguished Rock Climber, Royal Robbins.* Pat Ament,
Nebraska: Adventure's Meaning Press.
The Water People. Joe Simpson, London: Jonathan Cape.
(Alpine fiction)

1993   Winner: *The Ascent.* Jeff Long, London: Headline.
(Himalayan fiction)
This Game of Ghosts. Joe Simpson, London: Jonathan
Cape. (H197)
The Undiscovered Country: The Reason We Climb. Phil
Bartlett, Glasgow: The Ernest Press. (H13)

1994   Winner: *At The Rising of the Moon: Short Stories by ...*
Dermot Somers, London: Bâton Wicks. (H207)
Alps 4000: 75 Peaks in 72 Days. Martin Moran, Newton
Abbot: David & Charles.
Among Mountains. Jim Crumley, Edinburgh
Mainstream. (H65)
No Place to Fall: Superalpinism in the High Himalaya.
Victor Saunders, London: Hodder & Stoughton.

We Aspired: The Last Innocent Americans. Pete Sinclair, Utah State University Press. (Climbing in the Grand Tetons during the 1960s)

1995   Winner: *Geoffrey Winthrop Young: Poet, Mountaineer, Educator.* Alan Hankinson, London: Hodder & Stoughton. (H114)

Everest Calling: Ascent of the Dark Side: The Mallory-Irvine Ridge. Lorna Siggins, Edinburgh: Mainstream.

K2 The Story of the Savage Mountain. Jim Curran, London: Hodder & Stoughton.

The Burgess Book of Lies. Adrian & Alan Burgess, Seattle: Cloudcap. (H37)

Vertical Pleasure: The Secret Life of a Taxman. Mick Fowler, London: Hodder & Stoughton. (H88)

1996   Winner: *A Portrait of Leni Riefenstahl.* Audrey Salkeld, London: Jonathan Cape. (Biography of German film star/director)

A Spy on the Roof of the World. Sydney Wignall, Edinburgh: Canongate. (Himalayan climbing espionage in 1955)

Storms of Silence. Joe Simpson, London: Jonathan Cape. (Memoirs focusing on the Chinese/Tibetan conflict)

The Return of John Macnab. Andrew Greig, London: Headline. (H106)

1997   Winner: *Deep Play: A Climber's Odyssey from Llanberis to the Big Walls.* Paul Pritchard, London: Bâton Wicks. (H183)

Against the Wall. Simon Yates, London: Jonathan Cape. (Patagonian expedition)

Dark Shadows Falling. Joe Simpson, London: Jonathan Cape. (Exploring the issue of death in the mountains)

Icefields. Thomas Wharton, London: Jonathan Cape. (Canadian Rockies fiction)

Into Thin Air: A Personal Account of the Mount Everest Disaster. Jon Krakauer, London: Macmillan.
Spirits of Place: Travels, Encounters and Adventures in Wales. Jim Perrin, Llandysul: Gomer Press. (H177)

1998   Winner: *Eric Shipton: Everest and Beyond.* Peter Steele, London: Constable. (H212)
A Deathful Ridge: A Novel of Everest. J A Wainwright, Oakville: Mosaic Press. (H236)
Postcards from the Ledge: Collected Mountaineering Writings of ... Greg Child, Seattle: Mountaineers.
Sacred Mountains of the World. Edwin Bernbaum, University of California Press.
The Peak: Past and Present. Gordon Stainforth, London: Constable. (H211)

1999   Winner: *Totem Pole: And a Whole New Adventure.* Paul Pritchard, London: Constable. (Rehabilitation after a climbing accident in Tasmania)
Creagh Dhu Climber: The Life & Times of John Cunningham. Jeff Connor, Glasgow: The Ernest Press. (H54)
Ghosts of Everest: Authorised Story of the Search for Mallory and Irvine. Jochen Hemmleb, Larry A Johnson & Eric R Simonson, London: Macmillan.
High Achiever: The Life and Climbs of Chris Bonington. Jim Curran, London: Constable. (H70)
Regions of the Heart: The Triumph and Tragedy of Alison Hargreaves. David Rose & Ed Douglas, London: Michael Joseph. (H189)
Songs of Silence. Patricia Barrie, Dinas Powys: Honno. (H11)

2000   Winner: *The Wildest Dream: Mallory, His Life and Conflicting Passions.* Peter & Leni Gillman, London: Headline. (H96)

A Slender Thread: Escaping Disaster in the Himalaya.
Stephen Venables, London: Hutchinson.
Hell of a Journey: On Foot Through the Scottish Highlands in Winter. Mike Cawthorne, Edinburgh: Mercat Press.
(H46)
Travail So Gladly Spent. Tom Price, Glasgow: The Ernest Press. (H182)
White. Rosie Thomas, London: Heinemann.
(Himalayan climbing fiction)

2001 Winner: *Hazard's Way.* Roger Hubank, Glasgow: The Ernest Press. (H121)
Climbing Everest: A Meditation on Mountaineering and the Spirit of Adventure. Pat Ament, New York: Ragged Mountain/McGraw Hill.
Pyrenean High Route: A Ski Mountaineering Odyssey. John Harding, Wheathampstead: Tiercel Publishing.
Snow in the Kingdom: My Storm Years on Everest. Ed Webster, Eldorado Springs: Mountain Imagery.
The Middle-Aged Mountaineer: Cycling and Climbing the Length of Britain. Jim Curran, London: Constable. (H71)
Touching my Father's Soul: A Sherpa's Journey to the Top of Everest. Jamling Tenzing Norgay with Broughton Coburn, London: Ebury Press.

2002 Winner: *Fatal Mountaineer: The High-Altitude Life and Death of Willi Unsoeld, American Himalayan Legend.* Robert Roper, New York: St. Martin's.
Climbing Free: My Life in the Vertical World. Lyn Hill with Greg Child, London: Harper Collins.
Expeditions. Andrew Lindblade, South Barra: Hardie Grant. (Climbing memoirs)
Over the Edge: A True Story of Kidnap and Escape in the Mountains of Central Asia. Greg Child, London: Piatkus.

The Beckoning Silence. Joe Simpson, London: Jonathan Cape. (Memoirs leading to an ascent of the Eiger's North Wall)

The Evidence of Things Not Seen: A Mountaineer's Tale. W H Murray, London: Bâton Wicks. (H165)

Travels with the Flea: And Other Eccentric Journeys. Jim Perrin, Glasgow: The In Pinn. (H178)

2003   Winner: *The Fall*. Simon Mawer, London: Little, Brown. (H149)

Everest: The Official History. George Band, London: Harper Collins.

Mountains of the Mind: A History of a Fascination. Robert Macfarlane, London: Granta. (H138)

My Father, Sandy. Nicholas Wollaston, London: Short Books. (H256)

Tenzing, Hero of Everest: A Biography of Tenzing Norgay. Ed Douglas, Washington: National Geographic.

Yosemite: Half a Century of Dynamic Rock Climbing. Alexander Huber/Heinz Zak, London: Bâton Wicks.

2004   Winner: *When the Alps Cast Their Spell: Mountaineers of the Alpine Golden Age*. Trevor Braham, Glasgow: The In Pinn. (H28)

Feet in the Clouds: A Tale of Fell-Running and Obsession. Richard Askwith, London: Aurum Press. (H7)

Life and Limb: A True Story of Tragedy and Survival Against the Odds. Jamie Andrew, London: Portrait. (H5)

Nanda Devi: A Journey to the Last Sanctuary. Hugh Thomson, London: Weidenfeld & Nicolson.

With Friends in High Places: An Anatomy of Those Who Take to the Hills. Malcolm Slesser, Edinburgh: Mainstream. (H200)

2005   Joint winners: *Learning to Breathe*. Andy Cave, London: Hutchinson (H45) and *The Villain: the Life of Don Whillans.* Jim Perrin, London: Hutchinson. (H179)

Broad Peak. Richard Sale, Ross-on-Wye: Carreg. (First ascent controversy in 1957)

Mountain Rescue: Chamonix-Mont Blanc. Anne Sauvy. Bâton Wicks.

On Thin Ice: Alpine Climbs in the Americas, Asia and the Himalaya. Mick Fowler, London: Bâton Wicks.

2006   Winner: *An Afterclap of Fate: Mallory on Everest.* Charles Lind, Glasgow: The Ernest Press. (Poetic reconstruction of what might have happened)

A Rope of Writers: A Look at Mountaineering Literature in Britain. Graham Wilson, Disley: Millrace. (H251)

Breaking Trail: A Climbing Life. Arlene Blum, New York: Scribner.

High Endeavours: The Life and Legend of Robin Smith. Jimmy Cruickshank, Edinburgh: Canongate. (H63)

The Climbing Essays. Jim Perrin, Glasgow: The In Pinn. (H180)

2007   Winner: *The Wild Places.* Robert Macfarlane, London: Granta. (H139)

Brotherhood of the Rope: The Biography of Charles Houston. Bernadette McDonald, London: Bâton Wicks.

Happy Climbing Tells No Tales. Judith Brown, Cockermouth: Open Mountain. (H36)

Forever on the Mountain: The Truth Behind One of Mountaineering's Most Controversial and Mysterious Disasters. James M Tabor, New York: W W Norton.

Higher Than the Eagle Soars: A Path to Everest. Stephen Venables, London: Hutchinson. (H230)

The Mountains Look on Marrakech. Hamish Brown, Caithness: Whittles Publishing. (Atlas Mountains travelogue)

2008   Winner: *Psychovertical.* Andy Kirkpatrick, London:
       Hutchinson. (H132)
       Ararat. Frank Westerman, London: Harvill Secker.
       (Pilgrimage to Mount Ararat in Turkey)
       Cham. Jonathan Trigell, London: Serpent's Tail. (Alpine
       fiction)
       *Fallen Giants: A History of Himalayan Mountaineering
       from the Age of Empire to the Age of Extreme.* Maurice
       Isserman & Stewart Weaver, New Haven: Yale
       University Press.
       *The Eiger Obsession: Facing the Mountain that Killed My
       Father.* John Harlin III, London: Hutchinson.

Top Fifty Recommended Books

published before 1983 with British walking/climbing interest

The first edition is stated first, and then the most recent edition if it was republished later.

1. Abraham, A P: *Rock-climbing in Skye*. London: Longmans, 1908. Part 3 of the Jones–Abraham trilogy.

2. Abraham, G D: *Rock-climbing in North Wales*. Keswick: G P Abraham, 1906. Part 2 of the Jones–Abraham trilogy.

3. Baker, Ernest A: *Moors, Crags & Caves of the High Peak and Neighbourhood*. London: Fisher Unwin/Manchester: Heywood, 1903. (Tiverton: Halsgrove, 2nd facsimile edition, 2002.) Pioneer rock climbing in the Peak District.

4. Bell, J H B: *A Progress in Mountaineering: Scottish Hills to Alpine Peaks*. London: Oliver & Boyd, 1950. (*Bell's Scottish Climbs*. Leicester: Magma Books, 1995, abridged reprint.) Climbing instruction and memoirs.

5. Benson, C E: *Crag and Hound in Lakeland*. London: Hurst & Blackett, 1902. A mixture of rock climbing and the sport of fellside (fox) hunting.

6. Bonington, Christian: *I Chose To Climb*. London: Gollancz, 1966. (London: Weidenfeld & Nicolson, 2001, pbk.) His first autobiography.

7. Borthwick, Alastair: *Always a Little Further*. London: Faber, 1939. (London: Diadem, 1993, pbk.) Climbing in Scotland during the 1930s.

8. Brown, Hamish: *Hamish's Mountain Walk: the First Traverse of All the Scottish Munros in One Journey*. London: Gollancz, 1978. (London: Bâton Wicks, 1996, omnibus edition with *Climbing the Corbetts*.)

9. Brown, Joe: *The Hard Years: an autobiography*. London: Gollancz, 1967. (London: Phoenix, 2007, pbk.)

10. Byne, E & Sutton, G: *High Peak: the Story of Walking and Climbing in the Peak District.* London: Secker & Warburg, 1960.

11. Clark, Ronald W & Pyatt, Edward C: *Mountaineering in Britain: a History from the Earliest Times to the Present Day.* London: Phoenix, 1957.

12. Cleare, John & Collomb, Robin: *Sea Cliff Climbing in Britain.* London: Constable, 1973.

13. Coxhead, Elizabeth: *One Green Bottle.* London: Collins, 1951. (Reprinted in *One Step in the Clouds* by Salkeld & Smith, London: Diadem, 1990.) Climbing fiction based in Snowdonia.

14. Dent, C T: *Mountaineering.* London: Longmans, 1892. (3rd edition 1901 reprint.) Omnibus from the Badminton Library series featuring illustrations by H G Willink.

15. Frere, R B: *Thoughts of a Mountaineer.* London: Oliver & Boyd, 1952. Scottish climbing memoirs.

16. Gray, Dennis: *Rope Boy.* London: Gollancz, 1970. (1979 reprint.) Autobiography of Brown/Whillans contemporary.

17. Hankinson, Alan: *The First Tigers: the Early History of Rock Climbing in the Lake District.* London: Dent, 1972. (Keswick: Melbecks, 1984, pbk.)

18. Hankinson, Alan: *Camera on the Crags: a Portfolio of Early Rock Climbing Photographs by the Abraham Brothers.* London: Heinemann, 1975. (1979 reprint.)

19. Hankinson, Alan: *The Mountain Men: an Early History of Rock Climbing in North Wales.* London: Heinemann Educational Books, 1977. (Mara Books, 2004, pbk.)

20. Haston, Dougal: *In High Places.* London: Cassell, 1972. (Edinburgh: Canongate, 2003, pbk.) Autobiography.

21. Humble, B H: *The Cuillin of Skye.* London: Hale, 1952. (Glasgow: The Ernest Press, 2nd facsimile edition, 1986.) A climbing history.

22. Jones, Owen Glynne: *Rock-climbing in the English Lake District*. London: Longmans, 1897. (Manchester: Morten, facsimile reprint of 2nd edition, 1973.) Part 1 of the Jones–Abraham trilogy.

23. Kirkus, Colin: *Let's Go Climbing!* London: Nelson, 1941. (Ripping Yarns.com, 2004, pbk.) Instructional book and climbing reminiscences written for young people.

24. MacInnes, Hamish: *Call-Out*. London: Hodder & Stoughton, 1973. (1985, pbk.) Stories about the Glencoe Mountain Rescue Team.

25. Moffat, Gwen: *Space Below My Feet*. London: Hodder & Stoughton, 1961. (Wilmslow: Sigma Leisure, 2001, pbk.) Moffat was the first professional woman mountain guide in Britain. This was her first autobiography.

26. Moffat, Gwen: *Two Star Red: a Book about RAF Mountain Rescue*. London: Hodder & Stoughton, 1964.

27. Morin, Nea: *A Woman's Reach*. London: Eyre & Spottiswoode, 1968. Climbing memoirs from a prominent inter-war mountaineer.

28. Murray, W H: *Mountaineering in Scotland*. London: Dent, 1947. (Reprinted as *Mountaineering in Scotland/ Undiscovered Scotland*. London: Bâton Wicks, 1997, pbk.)

29. Murray, W H: *Undiscovered Scotland: Climbs on Rock, Snow and Ice*. London: Dent, 1951. (See above.)

30. Oppenheimer, Lehmann J: *The Heart of Lakeland*. London: Sherratt & Hughes, 1908. (Glasgow: The Ernest Press, facsimile edition, 1988, pbk.) Exploratory climbing in the Lake District around 1900.

31. Patey, Tom: *One Man's Mountains: Essays and Verses*. London: Gollancz, 1971. (Edinburgh: Canongate, 2005, pbk.) Posthumously published writings by well-known Scottish mountaineer.

32. Pilley, Dorothy: *Climbing Days.* London: Bell, 1935. (London: Hogarth Press, 1989, pbk.) Autobiography culminating with the first ascent of the north ridge of the Dent Blanche in 1928.

33. Poucher, W A: *The Magic of Skye.* London: Chapman & Hall, 1949. (London: Constable, 1989, pbk.) Mainly photography, focusing on the traverse of the Cuillin Ridge.

34. Pyatt, Edward C & Noyce, Wilfred (eds.): *British Crags and Climbers.* London: Dobson, 1952. An anthology of British mountaineering literature.

35. Rees, Lucy & Harris, Alan: *Take It to the Limit.* London: Diadem, 1981. Climbing fiction loosely based on Harris, who died in a car crash the year of publication.

36. Russell, Jean (ed.): *Climb If You Will: a Commentary on Geoff Hayes and his Club, the Oread Mountaineering Club.* EXPO/Rocksport, not dated [1974].

37. Sansom, G S: *Climbing at Wasdale Before the First World War.* Somerset: Castle Cary Press, 1982. Published on the 70th anniversary of the Pioneer Girdle Traverse of Scafell.

38. Smith, Roger (ed.): *The Winding Trail: A selection of articles and essays for walkers and backpackers.* London: Diadem, 1981.

39. Smith, W P H: *Climbing in the British Isles, Vol. 1: England.* London: Longmans, 1894, & *Vol. 2: Wales and Ireland* (by H C Hart). London: Longmans, 1895. The first guidebooks to British rock climbing.

40. Smythe, Tony & Cleare, John: *Rock Climbers in Action in Snowdonia.* London: Secker & Warburg, 1966. (1967 reprint.) Climbing personalities and photography.

41. Soper, Jack, Wilson, Ken & Crew, Peter: *The Black Cliff: the History of Rock-climbing on Clogwyn du'r Arddu.* London: Kaye & Ward, 1971.

42. Sutton, Geoffrey & Noyce, Wilfred: *Samson: the Life and Writings of Menlove Edwards.* Stockport: Cloister Press, not dated [1960].

43. Whillans, Don & Ormerod, Alick: *Don Whillans: Portrait of a Mountaineer.* London: Heinemann, 1971. (Harmondsworth: Penguin, 1976, pbk.) Autobiography.

44. 'Whipplesnaith' [Symington, N H]: *The Night Climbers of Cambridge.* London: Chatto & Windus, 1937. (Cambridge: Oleander Press, 2007.) Clandestine climbing on Cambridge University buildings.

45. Wilson, Ken (ed.): *Hard Rock: Great British Rock-Climbs.* London: Hart-Davis, 1974. (London: Diadem, 1992, 3rd edition.)

46. Wilson, Ken (ed.): *The Games Climbers Play.* London: Diadem, 1978. (1996, pbk. reprint.) Anthology of climbing magazine articles.

47. Wilson, Ken (ed.): *The Big Walks.* London: Diadem, 1980. (1990 reprint.) Challenging British mountain walks and scrambles.

48. Young, Geoffrey Winthrop (ed.): *Mountain Craft.* London: Methuen, 1920. (7th edition, 1954 reprint.) The classic mountaineering manual.

49. Young, G W: *Collected Poems of Geoffrey Winthrop Young.* London: Methuen, 1936.

50. Young, Geoffrey Winthrop, Sutton, Geoffrey & Noyce, Wilfred: *Snowdon Biography.* London: Dent, 1957. Climbing history and associated literature.

Book Search by Category

A customer asked me in the shop where I work part time, 'I'm looking for a book but I don't know what it's called and I've no idea who the author is.' The following index of titles listed under broad categories was created with this question in mind. Each book only appears under the category most closely matching its content. Some books defied our best efforts to categorise them, hence the Miscellaneous section at the end. The index number refers to the book number in the main bibliography list (H) or the Recommended Top Fifty (L), and not the page number.

CH

Autobiographies/memoirs contd.

Best of.../Selected articles

Mountain Rescue contd.

Countdown to Rescue (Snowdonia) H147

Mountain Rescue (Peak District) H124

Mountain Rescue (UK) H196

Rescue! (Lake District) H244

Sweep Search (Scotland) H142

The Black Cloud (Scotland) H219

The Price of Adventure (Worldwide/Scotland) H143

The Team (Lake District) H186

Two Star Red (RAF) L26

Whensoever (RAF) H43

Mountaineering literature

A Rope of Writers (Graham Wilson) H251

Mountaineering Literature (Jill Neate) H167

Mountains (where a mountain or area is the central theme)

After You, Mr Wainwright (Lakeland Fells) H160

Ben Nevis H61

Glencoe: Monarch of Glens H15

Glencoe: The Changing Moods H218

Lakeland H209

Mountain Lakeland H27

Mountaineering in Scotland L28

Scafell H22

Scotland's Mountains H164

Snowdon Biography L50

The Cuillin H210

The Life and Times of the Black Pig (Ben Macdui) H228

The Magic of Skye L33

The Peak H211

The Riddle of Sphinx Rock (Great Gable) H227

Undiscovered Scotland L29

Wainwright's Favourite Lakeland Mountains H234

Munro-bagging

A Measure of Munros H250

Burn on the Hill H2

Climbing the Corbetts H32

The First Fifty H103

The First Munroist H79

The Last Hundred H33

The Munro Phenomenon H76

Novels

A Deathful Ridge H236

Above the Horizon H52

Climbers H115

Fellrunner H135

Hazard's Way H121

In Kinder's Mist H68

Murder in the Glen H144

One Green Bottle L13

One Step in the Clouds (omnibus/ bibliography) H190

Songs of Silence H11

Take It to the Limit L35

Taking Leave H122

The Fall H149

The Long Day Done H187

The Return of John Macnab H106

The Round H223

Todhra H102

Photographic

Camera on the Crags (Abraham brothers) L18

Eyes to the Hills (Britain) H208

Short Title Index